I CRY IN CORNERS

I CRY IN CORNERS

Embracing Your Feelings,
THROAT-PUNCHING ANXIETY,
and Managing Your Emotions Well

CHARI OROZCO

Faith
Words

New York • Nashville

FaithWords
Hachette Book Group
1290 Avenue of the Americas, New York, NY 10104
faithwords.com
twitter.com/faithwords

First Edition: August 2023

FaithWords is a division of Hachette Book Group, Inc. The FaithWords name and logo are trademarks of Hachette Book Group, Inc.

The publisher is not responsible for websites (or their content) that are not owned by the publisher.

FaithWords books may be purchased in bulk for business, educational, or promotional use. For information, please contact your local bookseller or the Hachette Book Group Special Markets Department at special.markets@hbgusa.com.

Print book interior design by Bart Dawson

Library of Congress Cataloging-in-Publication Data

Names: Orozco, Chari, author.
Title: I cry in corners : embracing your feelings, throat-punching anxiety, and managing your emotions well / Chari Orozco.
Description: Nashville : FaithWords, 2023.
Identifiers: LCCN 2022057826 | ISBN 9781546004233 (hardcover) | ISBN 9781546004257 (ebook)
Subjects: LCSH: Emotions--Religious aspects--Christianity. | Emotional intelligence--Religious aspects--Christianity. | Jesus Christ--Example.
Classification: LCC BV4597.3 .O76 2023 | DDC 152.4--dc23/eng/20230405
LC record available at https://lccn.loc.gov/2022057826

ISBNs: 9781546004233 (hardcover), 9781546004257 (ebook)

Printed in the United States of America

LSC-C

Printing 1, 2023

To my loving and incredibly kind husband, who never stops holding my hand on the roller coasters of life. You are a pastor of pastors, a friend to everyone, and your pace reminds me of Jesus daily. This revelation is a testament of your love and patience.*

*Also, because when I told you I was dedicating the book to you, you said, "You better!"

———◆———

And to the loyal listeners of the podcast, who loved me in the corner long before these pages existed. This book is my love letter of gratitude to you. Love you, weirdos.

CONTENTS

THE INTRODUCTION

How to deal with crying in corners

Navigating emotions is hard; navigating emotions without Jesus *feels* impossible.

Cry in Corners started as a joke on Instagram. Someone asked me how I dealt with my emotions, and I replied, "That's easy; I cry in corners." They laughed, and I did not. Jesus cried in corners, and it was how I was actually working out my feelings.

That Instagram story spurred an idea to start a podcast about how to navigate being emotional in an emotional world inspired by the ways and truth of Jesus. So I jumped into the podcast world, all while keeping my day jobs of pastoring, writing, and creative directing. It's been a journey for sure, but it's been a journey that has taught me that emotions are a gift from God, and they are meant to be understood and stewarded well.

Sadly, I've acquired this revelation over years of navigating my emotions in unhealthy ways. For most of my life, I've been told that my emotions and my passions were too much, whether I was being ejected from a basketball game as a teenager or trying to speak up in a meeting about something I disagreed with. I've been told that my emotions were borderline offensive and that I needed to temper them if I ever wanted to be successful, if I ever wanted God to use my life.

Words matter, and these words spoken over my young heart and impressionable mind made me spiral. God's gift of a tender heart became calloused in that emotional spiral. As a young adult, I isolated myself from friends and family and went into the working world introverted and insecure. I then went into my marriage feeling unsafe, full of irrational fear and anxiety and way too easily angered. My twenties were spent with a skewed view of God formulated by people's perception of who I should be and what I should do with my emotions. And because I didn't know how to filter the opinions of others and my own broken perspective in a healthy way, my life and emotions became very difficult for me to navigate. Regardless of the circumstances, everything and everyone was a problem, and I was always the victim.

My calloused heart then produced a corrupted view of my

emotions and how to use them. Like everyone else who is told they are too much, I felt unworthy and unseen, and I cried in real corners on the regular. At one point I Googled "what to do when you feel depressed," and I went down the to-do list, and shocker, I was still depressed and overwhelmed by life afterward. The exercise didn't help, the no coffee made me sadder as coffee is of the Lord, and regardless of what I did, I still felt like I couldn't get a good grasp on my emotions. The Google search was an overall fail, and even though I was experiencing what everyone would deem personal and professional success, I still felt full of feelings, and I still felt like at any point I might explode. I tumbled out of my twenties and into my thirties, fearful, lonely, and still navigating emotions in an isolated and unhealthy way. I felt helpless. My boss at the time saw me struggling and suggested counseling, which offended me on a deep level. It didn't make me feel seen or valued that this person suggested counseling. It made me feel inferior and like others deemed me emotionally unstable.

Even though I wish therapy had been sold to me in a different package, I'm thankful for that moment. I needed counseling to be pushed upon me or I would have never gone. And my boss was right. I needed to be able to see myself and my emotions past what had been spoken over me. After several years of counseling, as well as seeking Jesus, I felt better and on the come-up. I was doing my devos every morning, and the Sunday church thing was all good!

I then experienced a few bouts of extreme burnout and a

couple of rounds of relational betrayal. Basically, I had zero boundaries and false expectations about community and friendships. All the therapy coping mechanisms seemed to vanish, so I went to more counseling sessions and continued to serve my local church.

Then I had a major emotional breakdown at the age of thirty-three. I'd done everything the world and the church told me to do to be whole, and yet I sat on the edge of my bed and contemplated taking my own life. There I was, happily married, working at what looked like a dream job in one of the fastest growing churches in the nation, sitting in rooms everyone wanted to be in, and I was miserable. I was lost in my emotions, and I couldn't find a way out. I needed Jesus, and not in a fifteen-minute devo or a churchy one-liner on social media kind of way. I needed the person of Jesus, the Prince of Peace, to walk into the room. I needed Jesus to step in and tell me what it looked like to truly be whole and to have healthy emotions. I needed Jesus to tell me I wasn't too much and that he could use my life even though everything about me screamed broken. And through the tears, I said, "Jesus, I know you're real, but I need you to be real right now."

And as those words left my lips, I felt the tangible presence of God hold me in that moment, and I knew I was going to be okay. Not because I went to church or called myself a Christian, not because I was in counseling sessions every week, but because Jesus had walked into the room, and I wasn't going to let him go.

The world has tons of remedies for wholeness, but I needed wholeness from the one who created me. I needed to experience wholeness, not as a destination I would arrive at one day but a road Jesus would walk me through daily. So I changed how I chased wholeness and healthy emotions. Not because the therapy was bad or because I stopped looking to professionals to give me guidance but because I was tired of allowing other people to tell me what they thought would make me better or more palatable to a broken world. I was tired of trying to fix *my* brokenness; I wanted to live in *Christ's* wholeness.

I knew I wanted to love God well, and love his people well, but I needed a clear way past all my feelings. So I took a deep dive into how Jesus navigated all the feels I was having, and how he responded. I needed to know how Jesus felt when he was betrayed or when he dealt with loss and disappointment. I needed to know if he'd ever felt lonely like me. Did he ever feel full of fear, and if he did, how did he respond? Did people ever think Jesus was too much, or was I all alone? If so, I needed a road map to navigating my emotions well. I needed the right tools to fight off anxiety, and I needed Jesus to walk me through it! Emotions are essential to who we are as human beings and who we are as followers of Jesus. They are the indicator lights that tell us something is wrong, and they are the spark plugs in our souls that ignite feelings of happiness, wonder, and awe. I found that Jesus experienced all the emotions and feelings you will ever have on a deep level, and he understood that in this temporal life, there will be a series of emotional corners that we can possibly get stuck in.

Have you ever been told that you were too sensitive, too emotional, or too much? How about too passionate, or too intense, or that you wear your heart on your sleeve? Yeah, me too. Nothing is more demoralizing to a person trying to pilot their feelings than constantly being told that their emotions are bad and can't be trusted. I'm not a therapist or a mental health specialist, but I have one of each. And I believe in getting extra help to navigate your feelings when life gets too hard or overwhelming. But what if, when life got tough, the help we ran to *first* wasn't our therapist, or friend groups, or social media? What if when life and emotions felt like they were trying to rob us of our peace, we ran to the Prince of Peace and asked him how to navigate it instead? What if we steered our feelings the way Jesus steered his?

Before you put this book down and roll your eyes: I know what I'm saying will feel like antiquated advice. I know that the advice to read scripture and seek Jesus in moments where life gets hard has been twisted and abused. I know this all too well as someone who has served in the local church for more than twenty years and currently pastors a community. But as the quintessential emotional person, I can say that even though I've seen the ways of Jesus being polluted and dumbed down, the ways of Jesus are still the only way: the only way to peace and the only way to true wholeness. The only way to really embrace your emotions well—all while throat-punching anxiety—is by navigating your feelings the way Jesus navigated his.

Before the days of online therapists, relaxation techniques, and medication, Jesus had to navigate difficulties and intense feelings. We see in the scriptures that when feelings got too real, Jesus turned to moments of solitude so he could hear his father's voice, the scriptures, and the power of the Holy Spirit. These things were how he navigated feelings of being overwhelmed, lonely, fearful, and anxious. He activated these things when life felt unsafe and when his identity was being shaken. He used these tools when he felt disappointment and betrayal and while dealing with unhealthy people and conflict. And this is how I also choose to live my life and how I navigate being an emotional being in a turbulent world where everyone has feelings about feelings and also about your feelings! When my emotions get to be too much, or I can't understand why I feel the way I feel, I go to Jesus first. When life gets too hard, I try to align my heart and mind to Jesus's ways and how Jesus modeled being an emotional being.

Have I always done it well? I mean, no. Not at all. I'm about to share how I royally screwed up living out the ways of Jesus because of my unhealthy emotions! But don't worry, I'm also going to pair it with how Jesus totally rocked at it. You're about to get a high-level perspective on managing your emotions well, but please note that I didn't write this book to fix our emotional brokenness. I wrote this book to inspire us into the fullness of all God has created us to be. And what he's created us to be is his voice of reason in the garden, his message of peace in the wilderness, and his expression of love from Gethsemane to Golgotha. You may find yourself crying in a corner every now and then, but be encouraged; so did Jesus. His life, regardless of those corners, inspired hope and freedom, and so can yours. That's my prayer for you, for us, to express the love, and the way of Jesus in all we do, especially in our emotions.

See you on the other side.

Onward.

CHAPTER 1

HIS VOICE

How to deal with feeling overwhelmed

If you don't know who you are,
your emotions will happily tell you.

I've never navigated being overwhelmed well. I'm not sure anyone besides Jesus ever has. Even now, in my forties, following Jesus, writing a book about feelings, and pastoring a church, the feelings associated with being overwhelmed stare me down. Fear, anger, worry, and helplessness seem to always be waiting in the wings for any sudden change I'm not ready for—a weird congregant email or a trigger from past trauma. And for clarity's sake, when I use the term *overwhelmed*, I define it as a level of stress that leaves me feeling emotionally stuck in my own personal quicksand with debilitating variations of hopelessness.

Being overwhelmed also causes me to feel buried or drowned, and to make matters worse, the feeling pushes me toward a not-so-Jesus-like response that usually looks like crying it out in the corner of my kitchen. But mostly, it looks like spending several hours or days in my nothing box, a cultivated space where I hide from all the things and people who are making me feel buried in feelings. My nothing box can also be defined as time spent rewatching movies based on Jane Austen classics while wearing my favorite sweatpants and sending out for Five Guys via DoorDash.

Full disclosure, when life gets overwhelming, I have a propensity to lose myself in unhealthy emotions and waste time. And when I say lose myself, I mean it's like I get amnesia about who I am and what I'm supposed to be doing. The things that are real and tangible and safe dissipate, and I get frozen in the moment; I get stuck. Stuck in unhealthy thought patterns. Stuck in speech that tears down my self-esteem and perspective, and stuck in hopelessness.

Imagine an astronaut who's been training for space for years. They've lived most of their adult life training their mind and body for space travel and exploration. And then they get to space and experience expectations not being met or a normal space problem, and they unravel. They forget how to spacewalk, how to navigate the no-gravity; they even forget that they are an astronaut and not some rando science nerd shot up into space as a joke. When I allow unhealthy emotions to lead my life instead of letting Jesus lead, I am that astronaut. Life gets overwhelming.

So overwhelming, in fact, that forgetting who I am becomes my default response. As a result, the only thing that defines me is whatever unhealthy emotion I've cultivated in the nothing box I have found myself in. And those emotions, which are usually pretty toxic, are then sprinkled on my hopelessness. Hopelessness is always the trigger for one of my infamous irrational panic attacks. And when the panic sets in, you can bet money that I will then try to abdicate whatever request or circumstance has made me feel overwhelmed.

My husband experienced this in the throes of a Disney World vacation early on in our marriage. I mean, he's been my best friend since we were fourteen, so he's seen my version of overwhelmed a few times. But not in public, not in the happiest place on earth.

Let me set this up: my husband is hands down the nicest person you will ever meet. He is walking sunshine with an Antonio Banderas accent and Jake Gyllenhaal eyes. Also, he lives in Hawaiian-style vacation shirts and is always telling dad jokes for no reason. The guy is a gem; we should protect him at all costs. He loves cooking breakfast and long walks on the beach. I can't make this stuff up, and to top it off, he is adored by everyone who meets him. He still holds my hand everywhere we go like we are teenagers dating. Honestly, he deserves a medal because I am, well, not like that at all. I am Eeyore from *Winnie the Pooh* with a dash of *Saturday Night Live*'s Debbie Downer. I am usually dressed in all black and wearing some form of fall attire, regardless of the season. Hats, boots, jackets for no reason, the whole nine yards. And this guy took me to Disney World on a whim because he is the greatest, and in response, I complained the entire time because I am a vampire and have issues with the sun. But I digress.

Have I mentioned yet that I have severe vertigo and don't like roller coasters? No, not yet? No worries—I have horrible vertigo and steer clear of roller coasters. But on this vacation, my husband must have forgotten that I hate roller coasters, dark tunnels, and places I could get stuck in and/or die while becoming a possible episode of *Dateline*. Pretty much anything that people deem fun or exciting is my worst nightmare. And on this particular day, my sunshine of a husband felt compelled to ride the Rock 'n' Roller Coaster, an enclosed super-fast ride of death. In my attempt to be a good wife, I reluctantly agreed to ride the coaster. He was so excited. You should have seen his face; his entire countenance lit up. And there we went; we stood in line sweating, and for some reason, I began to get excited; I was looking forward to experiencing this roller coaster with my husband. His joy and peace were infectious, and my entire attitude shifted right up until the moment they strapped me in.

That's when I realized I was now unable to get out, and this coaster was going to shoot me almost sixty miles an hour in 2.8 seconds into perpetual darkness! To say I was instantly overwhelmed in that moment would be an understatement. I thought I was all good, I was happy, I was safe, and then all those good feelings evaporated into thin air when the security bar locked into place. The certainty I felt in the line with my husband was now being replaced with an irrational fear that led me to a full-on panic, and I began to scream at the attendant, "Sir, can you let me off this ride!" My very lovely husband, to calm me down, took my hand gently, kissed it, and romantically whispered, "Everything is going to be okay because I'm here with you." And as he smiled and gazed into my crazy eyes, I yelled, "I don't care that you are here with me! What does that have to do with anything? Get me off this riiiiiiii—!" And before I could finish my words, the ride took off. I don't usually scream at strangers; that's not really my thing. But we do crazy things, irrational things, when we allow the feelings associated with being overwhelmed to take control of our lives.

Does anyone else have moments like this? Moments where everything is completely okay, and yet your fear of the unknown gets in the way of you experiencing something potentially amazing? I wish I could say this was the only time I've reacted like this, but it's not. And where this was a more comical variation of my panic, the truth is, I've responded like this more often than I care to admit to major life changes, people, and everything in between. And it's in these moments when my unhealthy emotions are reigning supreme that I run to the stories of the Bible to help me navigate the circumstances that push me to feel hopeless and fearful and ready to abandon those I love. The two stories I frequent when I'm feeling the most overwhelmed and hopeless are Eve's snake convo story found in Genesis 3 and Jesus's crying in the garden story found in the Gospels. Both Eve and Jesus faced situations that opened the door for them to question who they were and who they were following. One made an emotional decision that left humanity in need of a savior; the other came to earth to be that savior.

DON'T DO THIS

In Genesis, we find Eve in the garden, beautifully vulnerable, naïve, in love, and experiencing the creator in a supernatural way. Heaven had invaded earth, and Adam and Eve were physically walking with God. There was no shame, no sin, no stress or fear. I often wonder what it would have been like to live in that type of garden. Homegirl was stripped down emotionally and literally, and still, she was all good. I won't even wear shorts in public; this chick was naked and unafraid. On the small chance you don't know the story, I'm going to retell it, but you can also feel free to read the "non-Chari version" in Genesis 3:1–8. You're welcome!

Eve one day decided to take a stroll through the garden alone like I assume she'd done a bunch of times before, and she runs into the snake. Which the New International Version of the Bible calls "more crafty than any of the wild animals the Lord God had made." And by crafty, I don't mean the snake is frequenting Hobby Lobby and knitting hats; this guy is sketch city! Anyway, Eve all alone runs into Sir Sketch, and the snake begins to ask Eve a series of questions. In Eve's defense, the convo seemed innocent enough, except the snake wasn't trying to ask her how she was doing; he was out to steal her identity. His very first question, "Did God really say, 'You must not eat from any tree in the garden'?," was a setup. This is how I imagine the conversation going down.

Snake: Pssst, hey, girl!

Eve: *(looks around and then points at herself)*

Snake: That tree you're eating from sucks; you should eat from this tree. *(points at the forbidden tree)*

Eve: *(shakes head no)* That tree is forbidden.

Snake: Did God say that? That you can't eat from any tree in the garden?

Eve: *(says with her whole chest like a confident gangster)* Ugh, technically what he said was we can totally eat fruit from the trees in the garden, but God did say we can't eat fruit from the tree that is in the middle of the garden, and we can't touch it, or we will die.

Snake: Girl, please! You won't die. God knows that when you eat from it, your eyes will be opened, and you will be like God, knowing good and evil.

Eve: *(begins internal spiral and dialogue)*
Hhhuwhhhaaaaattt!
God is lying to me!
What does this thing mean I won't die?
Does God not trust me?
Why would he keep me from the truth?
Does Adam know?
Is Adam in on this sham of a garden situation?

This is so relatable. How many times have you walked into a situation with no backup, and someone asked you a question about something or someone you hold dear, and you just spiral? And by *spiral*, I mean hopelessness sets in, and you respond in words and in actions irrationally and out of character. You forget you're a grown-up with a mortgage or that you are the boss in the room. In these moments, I tend to forget that I'm a pastor! Eve did what I believe we all would have done and jumped off the emotional ledge. All she knew to be true seemed to vanish. She believed the worst-case scenario, which was that God the Father had somehow lied to her or that she wasn't given all the information she was due. Eve allowed her fear and confusion to replace who God said she was and what God called her to. Up to that point, all she knew was that she was a daughter of the creator, called to take care of God's creation, a super sweet gig that was supported by one-on-one time with the creator of the universe. And the snake, in one question, dismantled that entire belief system, and by the end of the conversation, instead of walking away to process her newfound feelings with the God who created her, she walked over to the tree, took the fruit, ate it, and gave it to Adam.

Eve was what I call new: new to the world, new to the struggle, new to people poking at what she believed, and at what perhaps others would call her truth. The enemy knew this well, and that is what he attacked. This is mind-boggling to me as this chick *walked with God*—like the creator of the universe was her walking buddy. I've heard it argued that the snake was just showing Eve that God wasn't totally telling her the truth. He was just shedding light on what God had kept in the dark. I mean, yes, technically, she wouldn't physically die if she ate the fruit, but she did die.

Her obedience died.

Her innocence died.

Her trust died.

Her perspective died.

And as a result, sin was given the breath of life.

In warning her away from that tree, God the Father was protecting Eve, just like any good father. He was strapped in the roller coaster of life next to her, holding her hand. And yet she was overcome with fear and confusion. Truth is, Eve had some real feelings she'd probably never really encountered until that conversation. No one has told me this; I'm not a theologian; I am just a Bible reader who has come to this conclusion based on Eve's response to the snake. I can imagine the internal dialogue in her head as the snake spoke to her. I have struggled with the same internal dialogue of forgetting who I am in overwhelming situations, especially in moments where everything I know to be true is shaken. And it's in this quicksand of feelings that I also forget that I am God's creation and fashioned in his image; I respond as Eve did.

Eve felt confused and unworthy of trust and communication. She felt betrayed by God, her faith, and her friendship. I mean, dang, that's relatable on a deep, deep level. And I understand all of it. So how do we guard our identity when a vast array of feelings is telling us the opposite of what God has said about us? What do we say to ourselves when hopelessness has set in, and we can't remember that being made in God's image means more than being a professional Christian? What happens when we forget that God created us with authority and mandate, and purpose, just like Eve?

Such great questions: I'm glad you asked. Well, you respond like Jesus did when he was in a similar situation.

DO THIS

Jesus is the greatest example of navigating emotions well. Even though he had every reason you could ever conjure up to unravel, he didn't get stuck or lose himself when he felt overwhelmed. Jesus didn't abdicate his calling or hide away in sweatpants. Jesus handled overwhelm and the stressors that led him into that feeling like a champ, throughout the various stories of the Gospels and in a corner at the garden of Gethsemane. This is where he modeled how to embrace his emotions and even feel overwhelmed without losing himself in his feelings. This is the story that we should all reference, especially in moments when we feel emotionally stuck in quicksand with debilitating variations of hopelessness.

The story kicks off in Matthew 26, and we find Jesus overwhelmed but not alone and stressed but not defeated. It's well into the night. Jesus is exhausted, and he knows he is just hours away from being arrested, betrayed, beaten beyond recognition, and abandoned by those he calls his friends and followers. Jesus has spent the weeks leading up to this moment trying to prepare his disciples for his departure. He's also been navigating verbal tussles with the religious elite and trying to process the knowledge that his life was going to come to a violent end. He is the Messiah, the Son of God, but he, in this moment, is also very human.

He is surrounded by olive trees, and he can see the city of Jerusalem off in the distance. This garden was a place of comfort that Jesus had visited and revisited countless times, but, on this night, it would be the setting of his betrayal and great sorrow. In Matthew 26:37, he tells his closest friends that he is sorrowful and deeply distressed. He then goes on to say, "My soul is overwhelmed with sorrow to the point of death. Stay here and keep watch with me." Jesus was facing the unknown, and like Eve, he felt crushed by whatever was next.

When Eve felt these feelings, she did not run to a place of comfort to pray with Adam. No, she had a convo with a snake, panicked, fell into sin, and took the whole world with her!

When Jesus was hit with that feeling, that crushing from the unknown, he did the absolute opposite. When Jesus was overwhelmed, triggered by stress, and facing feelings that caused him to feel disoriented, he told his friends, he told his heavenly Father, and then he surrendered all his feelings in the dust.

TELL SOMEONE

Jesus was the Messiah, the son of the Living God, purposed for sacrifice and love personified. If anyone had a firm identity and a hold on his emotions, it was Jesus. And yet, when the crushing feelings that preceded the cross overwhelmed him, he chose to set time aside to be in prayer to speak with his heavenly Father and also tell his friends that he was overwhelmed.

Take note: if you want to keep your identity intact, you must first tell someone who truly knows you that you are struggling. Jesus ran to the garden to pray to the most important voice in his life, his heavenly Father. But my own personal revelation of this moment is that Jesus, walking out this human life, knew that we tend to tell everyone else before we go to God. So he also took his closest friends with him to pray, to seek God, and to model how to deal with feeling overwhelmed.

For many of us, our default setting will be to tell our therapist or a pastor. Which isn't bad, but Jesus wasn't looking for an answer to the stress. Jesus wasn't looking for techniques or Bible verses he could use to help him feel less overwhelmed. He was looking for his closest friends to stand and pray with him. He was looking for support. Yes, even Jesus needed a support system. In my world, reaching out to my support system means a phone call to a trusted friend or a FaceTime with one of my siblings. It also means that I am going to have a sit-down with my husband and share with him whatever triggers have caused me to get stuck in quicksand, and then I will ask all of them to pray for me and with me. I ask them for their support, to reinforce the truth of who God says I am and not who my feelings say I am.

Some of you read that whole sharing your feelings thing and cringed, and others have already begun their three-hundred-word dissertation for social media. For the introverts reading this book who like to navigate their emotions alone in an introverted dungeon, be careful. Eve was alone, and it left room and opportunity for doubt and snake convos. You need people—I know, shocking! But it's true; you need to have people who know you well and can help you navigate your emotions with kindness and truth. I'm not saying to tell them all your business; actually, do not tell them all your sordid business. Just tell them enough that they will be adequately informed to lift you up in prayer or keep you accountable for making good life decisions.

Hey, extroverts, delete the social media post! Emotions should be surrendered to Jesus in private before they're vocalized to the public. This is not an opportunity for us to have crazy eyes and scare people with details over the metaverse. It's the complete opposite of that. We see Jesus at this garden moment modeling healthy accountability and wholeness. He models maturity, and he only shares his feelings with his inner circle, not the entire garden!

Read that again. Both who you tell and how you tell matter. But let's begin with who.

You have to tell the right people. The disciples were super tired as well and overwhelmed, so they went to sleep instead of locking arms with Jesus to pray. Don't tell your friends who are also super overwhelmed or riding the struggle bus. Tell people who you know have the bandwidth emotionally and the spiritual maturity to love you and see you through to step two. The last thing you need when you are overwhelmed is your homies napping on the job.

You may be asking, *Chari, are you saying Jesus wasn't aware that the disciples were going to fail him at that moment?* No, he totally knew, but I believe that Jesus chose to believe the best and took one on the chin so we could look back at this moment in Gethsemane and see the importance of navigating overwhelm with the right people.

How you tell people matters as well. Jesus encouraged his inner circle to pray with him as he spoke about his feelings. He was already showing them that his response to the feelings was prayer and time alone with his Father. He didn't tell them so they could be the answer to all his problems but to ask them instead to lock arms with him as he sought the answers in prayer. The focus was prayer, not the problem. Not his emotions, but prayer. When you tell your inner circle about your feelings with prayer locked and loaded, it helps you stay focused on who God says you are instead of what the problem or your feelings say you are.

He is also setting us up for a win, because if we somehow forget to walk out step two, those whom we've confided in will kindly remind us that it is only in step two that we get a refresher on who we are.

GET HONEST

After Jesus tells his friends how he's feeling and encourages them to pray, he then walks away to get on his face and have a one-on-one with his Father. This step is so crucial in holding on to who you are when overwhelm is the loudest song on life's playlist. It's important because who you are isn't made up of pieces of your personality or preferences. Who you are isn't what you do, what you love, or what you produce. Who you are is attached to whose you are. And when you walk with

God, when you say yes to Jesus, you become an heir to the Kingdom. You become a son or daughter of the Living God, and no amount of snake convos, fear, betrayal, or hopelessness can change that. Jesus was God's son, which meant he had access to peace and comfort in the darkest of moments. Yet, in the garden, the Gospel of Luke describes Jesus as being in such agony, such stress, that in the garden of Gethsemane, his sweat became like drops of blood falling down to the ground.

Can you imagine praying so hard for an answer, pleading for comfort, or being so overcome by sorrow that you sweat blood? I cannot, but Jesus was experiencing a level of stress that, thankfully, most of us will never have to endure. And in that stress, and in that quicksand of overwhelm, he prayed, "Father, this is the last thing I want. If there is any way, please take this bitter cup from Me" (Matthew 26:39 VOICE).

Let's pause here and look at this conversation, as it was honest, raw, and vulnerable. Jesus knew who he was and who he could run to in moments of overwhelm. His father was a safe place to say what he felt and a mirror that reflected Jesus's purpose and identity. So he prayed and prayed until he ran out of words. He prayed and prayed until an angel, as we're told in Luke 22:43, came and comforted him. And then once he was comforted, he prayed some more, as comfort pauses the struggle and allows you a moment to center your heart and mind back on God. But prayer, it's what will ultimately propel you forward in the struggle.

Have you ever prayed like that? In moments when you feel like you're drowning, have you ever prayed until the words vanished and you were swallowed up in comfort? What a prayer life this must have been, the type of prayer life that moves you toward God and away from despair in the worst moments. I sometimes wonder what would have happened if Eve had paused and run back to the Father with the same vulnerability and honesty that Jesus modeled for us. Would her story have been different? I then wonder what our lives would look like in moments where we feel buried by emotions, if we unleashed our hopes and dreams and concerns on our creator.

Jesus was crying in a corner, but it wasn't like ugly crying without purpose. It was a cry that said, *I need comfort, I need my Father, and I need a way forward.* It was a pursuit that I'm certain had been done many times before, as when all else failed and his friends kept falling asleep, Jesus did what he'd been doing for thirty-plus years: he surrendered his tears and emotions to the plans and purposes of his Father.

LET GO

After Jesus realized his friends were going to sleep through the struggle, he went back to his heavenly Father one last time and prayed, "Father, if there is no other way for this cup to pass without my drinking it—not My will, but Yours be done" (VOICE). In moments when life feels the most over-whelming, I tend to hold on to the roller coaster, close my eyes, say words I'm not proud of, and panic. Jesus, unlike me, lifted his hands on the ride and just surrendered his life and emotions to the Father and the Father's will for him. He didn't forget that he was the son of the most-high God. He didn't forget he was purposed to redeem the snake convo and major fail from the first garden. He didn't forget. And so he pressed forward, with a surrendered heart and mind.

Letting go doesn't mean you've given up, that you've lost in the struggle, or that you are weak. Letting go means you're human and in need of a savior. And Jesus knew at this moment he would need his Father to guide him through the horrific moments he was about to endure.

What would life look like if you did the same? What would it look like if you let go of whatever stressor was burying you and laid it down? When unhealthy emotions begin to bury you and circumstances overwhelm you, ask God for his will to be done and ask him to reveal what that will look like. In this Jesus story, it looked like shaking off the dust, wiping away tears, and bracing himself for what was next. Letting go may be like that for you as well.

Practically speaking, letting go could look like shaking off a relationship. For other situations, it may look like going to work even though your boss isn't your favorite, or it's not your dream job, but it pays your bills and supports your family. This could also look like forgiveness for some and heavy boundaries for others. But letting go, like Jesus, looks like saying yes to moving forward even when you don't know what the outcome is. It's saying, *I don't need the details that show me the way forward; I just need to know, God, you are with me.* But that is how Jesus walked out, an overwhelm that left him sweating blood. He said, "Not My will, but yours be done."

When I'm the most overwhelmed and I have my support system praying, and I'm personally praying and seeking God until I've lost words, I find that I begin to let go of:

- Unhealthy words about myself or the circumstance.
- Unhealthy expectations about what I'm facing.
- All expectations about how I'd like to see the situation work out.

And then I replace those things with life-giving Psalms or Proverbs about who God is. Regardless of the circumstance I find myself in, regardless of how overwhelmed I feel, the truth is always the same. God is with me, and he will get me through. It's not that my feelings are not valid or worthy of processing; it's just that my feelings that are not surrendered to God in prayer become unhealthy and drown me instead of pushing me forward. I'm not saying prayer is a replacement for wise counsel, a good ol' therapy appointment, or medicine. I'm just saying when my emotions are running amok, I choose Jesus as my first response and not my last resort. What would that look like if you did the same?

CHOOSE YOUR GARDEN

These two stories are my north and south on the compass of my emotions. One is my true north, and the other is my south, full of hurricanes, scary news stories, and loose gators. In the first story, Eve alone ran to the forbidden fruit instead of running to God with what was making her feel so overwhelmed. She, like many of us, let her hopelessness, confusion, and fear of the unknown be her guide. And when she did, the world imploded.

In the second story, Jesus made sure he had friends praying for him and with him, and he then went to the Father and asked the questions in need of answers. And when he did, the world was restored.

Feelings are a powerful pull, but don't let them pull you into isolated walks in the garden or convos with snakes. Instead, do as Jesus did: keep your community close by, and only share your feelings with those who can lock arms with you in prayer and in purpose. Seek the Father for wisdom regularly, as he is God enough for your questions, emotions, and lack of understanding. And if needed, let go. God's will for you is bigger and better than you could ever imagine. Will that mean you will have to crucify some expectations? Yes, probably, but freedom and wholeness are on the other side of your letting go.

Jesus experienced the same kind of feelings we do every day. And on that night in his favorite garden, when the security bar strapped him into what was next, he didn't allow his overwhelming grief to detour him from wherever the roller coaster was going to take him. He embraced the garden, even though he may have felt scared or sad. He chose to trust God in the process, and that, my friends, is how we should respond, always. The way of Jesus may have you crying in corners, but it's a safe corner. A corner full of God's presence and comfort. Here's to crying in more garden corners, as these corners keep us standing strong and with integrity when we are persecuted. They keep us loving and seeing people when life feels crucified, and they bring freedom and healing to our world.

Don't panic.

Embrace the roller coaster.

Tell the right people.

Let go if needed.

You are not alone.

Onward.

CHAPTER 2
HIS PRESENCE

How to deal with feeling lonely

---

*Alone with God isn't a lid
on your life; it's shade.*

I have found that crowded rooms trigger loneliness in me: the type of rooms that are filled with small talk and niceties and topics I can't dive into with total understanding. I also feel lonely when I'm misunderstood or can't communicate effectively. Loneliness, or the distressing feeling that blurs emotions and perspective on my quality of life and relationships, is blinding. I sometimes blame this feeling of loneliness on my introversion or the processing deficit that doesn't allow me to recognize or interpret information correctly. But the truth is that in moments where I am laser-focused on my deficiencies and triggers and not focused on who God is and who God says I am—those are the moments when loneliness tends to blind me.

Feeling blind isn't a new thing for me because without my glasses or contacts, I can only really see about five inches in front of me. Everything else is a total blur. I can't drive; I can't read signs; I can't differentiate who's in front of me. When I'm not wearing my glasses, I've been known to greet the wrong people, completely miss steps, and on occasion trip over curbs. One time I went to put on my glasses and didn't see the toothpick I was holding in my hand and may or may not have poked myself in the eye. I can't make this stuff up. This is why I have various kinds of contacts and glasses to make sure my 20/20 is locked down. I have different glasses for outside, for events, for specific outfits, and for everyday work. I have contacts that last two weeks, and some that last four weeks. And one time I had contacts that changed my eye color to blue! I care a lot about my vision, and so it's something I invest time and money into as I want to live this life out with a clear perspective.

One time I thought my vision had been miraculously healed. I woke up one random morning and stumbled to the bathroom to put in my contacts, and I couldn't find them. So

I grabbed a new set, popped them in, and to my surprise, I couldn't see. Everything was blurry. Confused, I took my contacts out, cleaned them, and put them in again—still blurry. I removed them once again and began to reclean them when all of a sudden, I realized I could see. Like, perfectly! I popped my head out of the bathroom and into the hallway to make sure I wasn't hallucinating, and sure enough, your girl had 20/20 vision!

I started to get teary-eyed and began a "thank you, Jesus, I've been healed" monologue when reality hit. The tears had dislodged something, and I could then feel there was something already in my eye. Yep, you may have guessed it. The night before, I fell asleep in my contacts, and that morning I forgot I had them already plastered to my eyeballs, and I put a new set on top of them. I wasn't healed from my extremely blurred vision; I had forgotten that I already had everything I needed in place to see things correctly. I just needed to rehydrate them with the right solution. But what is the right solution for the blurriness loneliness causes? Is it perhaps a fresh relationship or a new job? Is it self-isolation or removing all the blurry objects and just doing life alone? In all my searching and mistakes, I've landed on the following truth: there is no clear path away from loneliness without Jesus guiding the way.

As a result of this truth, I battle feeling rejected or lonely by getting alone and removing any voices or influences that may take my focus off seeing things the way Jesus sees them.

My solution to loneliness is solitude with my creator instead of isolation with my feelings. This solitude rehydrates my soul, my perspective, and my mind. And because I know the outcome is always a clear vision, I intentionally fill my time, especially my alone time, recharging my mind and my heart with who God is and who God says I am. This deliberate hiding away and shift of my vision also gives me time to process any struggles I have had in my day and centers my focus off the day and back to fully on God.

What makes you feel isolated and lonely? Is it crowds, like for me, or is it maybe the opposite? Can you articulate the circumstances or steps that lead you to loneliness and how you personally navigate it? Take a moment and write down those answers on the edges of this page or in a journal. If you don't know what triggers your loneliness, you won't be able to guard your heart and mind against those moments with healthy and life-giving responses and emotions.

When I catch wind of loneliness tossing me a new pair of contacts, I deliberately find a space or moment to hide away and pray. Sometimes I'll listen to worship music and read my Bible. I will even go sit in my car for thirty minutes on my lunch break. On other days I just simply close the door to my office so I can hit a hard reset on my feelings. Intentional hiddenness is something I embrace and something I endorse as it helps with loneliness and working out life. I also use moments of intentional hiddenness to read books that encourage my heart and mind, and in some instances, I embrace the beauty of doing nothing. No agenda. No phone. No emails. Just an empty slate for Jesus to speak to me.

I do this hiding away not just when I'm feeling lonely but as a preemptive strike against potential loneliness. I hide away daily, and I do this in an extreme form on Saturdays. Alicia Britt Chole, an author I respect greatly, calls it the "Sacred Slow, an unhurried honesty before God." And it's in that sacred slow, this purposeful hiddenness where I cultivate healthy solitude and have honest conversations with myself and God. This type of solitude combats my feelings of loneliness by refocusing my mind on the truth of God's word so that I can filter my emotions in a healthy way. It's where my healthy emotions like joy and peace and patience are refined in my life. The type of healthy fruit of the spirit-led emotions that shift the words coming out of my mouth and the sarcasm-laced reactions on my face. It's in this hiding away that I am able to redirect my mind away from what loneliness says about me and toward what God says about me. This hiding away also cleans my emotional glasses of fear and frustration and keeps the feeling of being overwhelmed and lonely far, far away.

Solitude—or as I call it, healthy hiddenness—is a Kingdom thing, an absolute Jesus thing that we as followers of the way should desire deeply and walk out intentionally. But since Eve decided to go all vegan, sin and brokenness corrupted solitude and replaced it with isolation. And isolation, solitude's weirdo cousin, does not produce joy and peace. It creates a padded cell of loneliness, doubt, and mistrust. And if not remedied quickly, it can cause us to feel undervalued, unseen, and disregarded. And what forty-plus years of life and twenty-plus years of serving people in some form of ministerial role have taught me is that I must be devoted to solitude, the type of solitude that's rooted in intentional hiddenness with Jesus.

So if you are feeling lonely or have ever felt abandoned or isolated, well, ironically, you are not alone. Many people feel isolated and abandoned by relationships and circumstances—even people in the Bible. And after all my Bible digging, I can't definitively say Jesus himself felt lonely, but I do know there were moments when he could have and should have felt alone and isolated. And if I had to bet on it, I'd say Jesus navigated feeling lonely more times than we can imagine.

Yes, Jesus was the Son of God, the Messiah, but he was also human, just like us, and navigating situations that could make him feel lonely, just like us.

Jesus was overlooked (John 1:46).

Jesus was rejected (Matthew 21:42).

Jesus was abandoned (Mark 14:50).

Jesus felt forsaken (Matthew 27:46).

Jesus was just like us, and the Bible tells us Jesus modeled healthy solitude in the midst of lonely moments that could have catapulted him into unhealthy isolation and a blurred perspective. Throughout the Gospels, we see that Jesus did two very specific things that helped him navigate all the moments in which loneliness could have blurred his vision.

First, he intentionally chose to hide away to focus on his

personal growth, as loneliness can't grow in the soil of Godly confidence. And second, he engaged the Holy Spirit in his daily walk. Jesus did these two things because he knew that we fight loneliness with maturity cultivated in hiddenness and emotions found in the Holy Spirit. And he also knew that the other side of that prayer-focused solitude would be a sharp perspective and healthy spirit-led emotions that would have the power to sucker-punch loneliness's blinding ways.

JESUS LONELINESS HACK 1: EMBRACE HIDDENNESS

Jesus spent most of his ministry life navigating all kinds of feelings, people, wins, losses, and traumatic scenarios that were then met with him slipping away to pray and be alone with his heavenly Father. Jesus was a poster child for embracing solitude in moments that felt and looked isolating, and that could have triggered feelings of loneliness. On top of solitude and devoting time to prayer, he also spent a good portion of his life in various forms of actual hiddenness. I define these moments as *seasons of anonymity our creator uses to hide us away for personal growth*. For example, think about the nine to ten months most of us spent in the womb, hidden, growing, yet safe. That's hiddenness. When you were in the womb, people knew you were there, but you were just tucked away, not ready to be unleashed on the world. And I believe these seasons of anonymity or hiddenness cultivated Jesus's ability to navigate loneliness by teaching him the importance of hydrating his perspective with solitude.

Before Jesus appears on the scene to save the world in his thirties, he is safely tucked away. Yet, at the age of twelve, we get a small glimpse into his pre-ministry life. That glimpse is found in Luke 2, and it kicks off like this. Every year Jesus's family would head to Jerusalem to celebrate Passover. This year was no different. They went, they celebrated, and when the festivities were all said and done, the family packed up and hooked up with the caravan to head back to Nazareth, where they lived. About a day into the trek home, Jesus's parents realized they couldn't find him. They assumed their firstborn was somewhere within the caravan, but he wasn't. They franticly searched for Jesus, and when they realized he was not there with the caravan, they journeyed back to Jerusalem to find him. It took them three whole days to find Jesus, but when they finally found him, he was just chillin' in the temple, without a care in the world.

Let me just interject: if Jesus's mom, Mary, had been Latina, there would not have been any talking or asking why he was in the temple when she found him. Just a slow-motion flip-flop flying through the air and a beating that would have lasted through the trek back to Nazareth.

But that wasn't what happened. Jesus was "in the temple courts, sitting among the teachers, listening to them and asking them questions" (Luke 2:46). People were in awe and amazed by Jesus. They were astonished by how he spoke and asked questions; his parents were not as impressed and scolded him. "Son, why have You treated us this way? Listen, Your father and I have been sick with worry for the last three days, wondering where You were, looking everywhere for You" (Luke 2:48 VOICE). Jesus then famously responds that he was about his Father's business, duh! Mary and Joseph were confused, yet in verse 51, the Bible says he went back to Nazareth obediently.

Now, was Jesus lonely, or feeling lonely in the temple? Probably not. He was probably living his best twelve-year-old life. A twelve-year-old in ancient Israel was not a kid, but he was becoming a man. And we should note that all the triggers that could possibly make him feel lonely were back in Nazareth. First off, Nazareth was the hood, and the trek back was going to be rough without that caravan. Also, when they did get to Nazareth, there were people there who were totally whispering about who Jesus's real daddy was. He was also a big brother to half-siblings who didn't really understand him. And there's a massive chance the neighborhood kids were probably making fun of him on the regular as Jesus and his family were not wealthy, and his birth story isn't one you'd want to post on social media. Yet, Jesus returned to Nazareth obediently.

I battle my lonely feelings with solitude. Solitude tucks me away, shifts my perspective, and then releases me back into the rooms and circumstances that once made me feel lonely. It's like a cycle that moves from circumstances to solitude, from solitude to perspective, and then it circles back around to whatever circumstance caused me to feel lonely. But the next go-round, the triggers that once blurred my perspective on my quality of life and relationships are not as triggered, or not triggered at all. And the Jesus in the temple, the Jesus who forgot—or didn't think it necessary—to tell his parents he was staying behind was not ready to be thrown back into the room. He needed solitude. He needed a few more rounds with Nazareth before he could successfully face Gethsemane and, ultimately, Golgotha.

The book of Luke says that after he went home, "Jesus grew in wisdom and stature, and in favor with God and man." Jesus, at twelve, knew that he wasn't ready to be unleashed on the world. He knew he needed to grow more, mature more, and work through his loneliness triggers in the safety of his parents' home and shade before he'd have to navigate them in the wilderness alone. Jesus at twelve was awesome, but Jesus at thirty-three changed the world. And so we see Jesus heading back to Nazareth and stepping into a moment where his heavenly Father needed him to hide away for more growth, and he did it obediently.

Next time you are in a situation or season where loneliness begins to creep in, what would happen if you chose solitude with your creator to remind you of the truth that loneliness blurs? The truth is that he is always with you, and you are never alone! What would life look like if you obediently chose to hide away to ask God what blurred your vision and caused you not to see yourself the way God sees you? What happened to make you forget that you were not alone in the room and that the creator of the universe was with you, always?

Practically speaking, if you want to cultivate a Jesus-like immunity to loneliness, you must first embrace the Jesus-type hiddenness, obediently and periodically, to mature you and sharpen your perspective. Jesus learned over the years that getting to be alone with God the Father to recharge, regroup, and refocus was what he needed to do to be unleashed on the world. Whatever greatness was in him still had to be incubated with a mature perspective and more time with God the Father. I understand this on a granular level, as I was born premature and lived in an incubator for the first three months of my life. Some of us will get to choose solitude to combat our loneliness and its triggers, while others will be gently nudged into it. Whichever variation of healthy hiddenness you are currently facing, do it with obedience, because if you do, maturity and favor will meet you on the other side of that solitude.

Combating loneliness by taking time to hide away to hear from God may feel and sound backward. I get it; spending time alone with God so you don't feel lonely sounds upside-down. But I'm not asking you to spend time alone; I'm asking you to spend time alone with God. There's a big difference. You alone without Jesus will cultivate loneliness. You alone with Jesus will cultivate solitude, and it's that solitude that will keep you with a sharp perspective. The type of perspective that will love people well and walk into rooms and circumstances with confidence in God and who God says you are. But when that loneliness cycle comes back around—and it will come back around—you'll meet that feeling with healthy emotions and maturity cultivated in the presence of your creator. That reminds you that you are a child of God, that you have been created for a purpose and on purpose, and that God will *never leave you or forsake you.*

JESUS LONELINESS HACK 2: POWER UP ON THE HOLY SPIRIT

Fast-forward twenty-plus years, and Jesus shows up in his thirties after intentional healthy hiddenness has made him a force to be reckoned with. In Matthew 3, Jesus walks out of the hiddenness that grew his favor and maturity to get baptized by the prophet and well-known weirdo John the Baptist. For context's sake, and because I think this story is dope, just know that when John the Baptist shows up on the scene, it has felt very much like God has been silent to the Jewish people for the past four hundred years. Four hundred years since a prophet spoke God's words from heaven. It had been four hundred years since the Old Testament, which felt like God had left his chosen people on read. And out of nowhere, in the middle of the Roman occupation of Judea, comes a prophet—the kind of prophet who had Old Testament prophecies that scared the living crap out of the religious and non-religious alike. This prophet lived in the desert, ate locusts and wild honey, dressed in camel skin, and picked fights with religious people!

And then Jesus shows up, and this prophet who had been preparing the way for Jesus immediately gets the memo that his portion of the job is now done, and Jesus is going to take it from here. They have an incredible moment, and Jesus gets baptized; it was game-changing. There are doves, and the voice of God thunders from the heavens and affirms that Jesus is indeed the Messiah. It's one of those "you had to be there" moments.

Jesus getting baptized would be the equivalent of that golden buzzer thing going off on that show *America's Got Talent*. There is a buzzer they push that validates the singer or the person who's got talent. That buzzer means they don't need to be judged or given feedback, and it immediately pushes them to the front of the line. Gold confetti falls from the sky, people are clapping and crying, and everyone feels like they have discovered this hidden gem.

That's what that moment felt like for everyone watching Jesus get baptized. But in the story of Jesus, there was no record deal after his big discovery moment; there was no Vegas show he was about to headline. Just another round of the life cycle for Jesus to possibly feel lonely, embrace solitude, gain a heavenly perspective, and get thrown back into the room. There was a lot on the line for Jesus. People to be saved and healed, and snake convos needing to be restored.

He didn't have time to sit around and enjoy the moment; he needed to get alone with his heavenly Father and regroup, refocus, and reset his mind and heart for whatever was next. And what was next would be powerful.

Even though Jesus had this amazing season of hiddenness, and his favor and ability to navigate loneliness had matured, there was an aspect to his life that still had to be activated so that life and busyness and storms and trials and people would not shake his emotions into unhealthy responses. We find this activation in Matthew 4. In a nutshell, Jesus gets baptized after years and years of hiddenness, and you'd think he'd be done with having to navigate being alone and feeling lonely, right?! Nope. After he gets baptized, the story abruptly shifts: "The Spirit then led Jesus into the desert to be tempted by the devil. Jesus fasted for 40 days and 40 nights" (VOICE).

Jesus has spent his entire life in relative hiddenness and then finally gets a golden buzzer, and the Holy Spirit, in response, chooses to lead Jesus into a desert to be tempted, all alone. Like very much alone, where every bit of loneliness and lost perspective could be roaming along with the devil! I'm going to unpack this story in the next chapter because it's a lot, but the part I want to land on here is this: after forty days and nights of more hiddenness and aloneness and verbal tussles with the enemy that could have very much blurred Jesus's emotions and perspective on his quality of life and relationships, Jesus walks out of that desert in the power of the Holy Spirit.

Let me say it again for those who glanced right over that. Jesus goes into the wilderness alone, led by the Spirit, obediently. Kind of like the one time he had to go back to Nazareth obediently. But this time he doesn't just walk away with favor and maturity. He walks away with the power of the Holy Spirit. I can imagine this moment is a bit like Jesus walking out of the desert with explosions behind him in slow motion, and the intro to "Sweet Child O' Mine" by Guns N' Roses is playing in the background! The power of the Holy Spirit, fam! The power that will feed the five thousand, and heal the sick, blind, and lame. The power that will keep him moving after betrayal, arrest, beatings, and crucifixion. The power that will fight death and win.

Just like with the gentle nudge in the temple that said solitude was needed, the Holy Spirit led him *into* more hiddenness. And then the Spirit walked him *through* the hiddenness, and when Jesus got to the end, he was walking in *power*. If you want to combat loneliness and the blurriness it causes, you must not only embrace hiddenness that matures you in a safe space but hiddenness that equips you and activates the power of the Holy Spirit in your life, in your words, and in your emotions. Life is hard and full of emotions and lonely moments, and it's even harder to navigate when you are not walking out of your life in the power of the Holy Spirit.

Galatians 5:22–23 encourages us to walk with the Holy Spirit like Jesus did. "The Holy Spirit produces a different kind of fruit: unconditional love, joy, peace, patience, kindheartedness, goodness, faithfulness, gentleness, and self-control" (VOICE). And if we allow the Holy Spirit to be activated in our lives, it produces fruit in our lives. And this fruit in action looks like healthy emotions that will help us navigate treks back to Nazareth to mature us and scary wilderness scenarios that we have to go into alone, preceded by a weirdo and eventual meet-ups with an enemy. I said earlier that solitude without Jesus is just you hanging out with yourself alone; it's awkward isolation. But when the Holy Spirit is activated in your life, it will keep you seeking after good fruit when you're alone. It keeps you moving toward fruit bearing solitude, and then healthy perspective. It will shift your potential bouts of isolation into fighting off those loneliness triggers like a boss. This fruit, cultivated in walks and talks with the Holy Spirit, will look like love, joy, peace, patience, kindness, goodness, faithfulness, gentleness, and self-control. And these fruits, if you allow them to grow and develop correctly, will fight off loneliness and its blurry effects.

BE LOVE

You can't feel lonely if you're saturated in the love of God. Love is the ability to see and care for people like Jesus did without needing affection or admiration in return. I have found that love cultivated and experienced in God's presence allows us to see and care for people the way God sees and cares for them. It keeps us from losing our perspective in moments of hiddenness or awkward rooms filled with small talk. Love is so beyond a feeling or a version of extreme liking; in the Kingdom it's a way of seeing the world and accepting people unconditionally and in a healthy way. It walks you back to Nazareth with a good attitude, and it keeps you chasing solitude with the Father, because without it, your perception of love, people, and feelings will get blurry. And it's love, powered by the Holy Spirit, that reminds us that in loneliness we are never truly alone.

CHOOSE JOY

You can't feel lonely if you're filled to the brim with the joy of the Lord. Joy is the feeling of immense happiness that isn't thwarted by temporal circumstances and is rooted in gratitude. This feeling is long-lasting and doesn't produce fleeting moments of happiness, because it is always thankful. See, happiness is a fleeting feeling, and it is thankful when things are good; joy is something that lasts, and its gratitude doesn't wane. Also, that joy powered by the Holy Spirit can find happiness and gratitude even in the most lonely scenarios—even when you're in a desert, hidden and alone. We see that Jesus would need this joy, as life was about to get super hard, and his perspective had to be sharp with long-lasting joy. The apostle Paul, in the book of Hebrews, explained that Jesus's perspective was joy: "For the joy set before him he endured the cross, scorning its shame, and sat down at the right hand of the throne of God." Joy is not a person or a place. It's fulfilling God's will for your life; it's living sacrificially because you know people will experience freedom through your joy. What does this have to do with loneliness? If you are walking out your life in the power of the Holy Spirit, filled with peace and love and joy, there will be no room for loneliness, as the Spirit will fill every crevice of your heart and mind.

WALK IN PEACE

You can't feel lonely if you're walking with the Prince of Peace. Peace is more than feeling tranquil; it's walking in confidence, soundness of mind, and completeness only found in solitude with God. Peace helps you navigate things and people and circumstances beyond your understanding. Also, peace—that type of peace powered by the Holy Spirit—doesn't disappear when everyone betrays you and when loneliness and fear try to creep in. It's a firm foundation and it has the power to change your lives, your atmospheres, your relationships, and your view of hiddenness.

BE CONSISTENTLY PATIENT

You can't feel lonely if you're navigating life with patience.
Patience is less about waiting, and more about *how* you wait
and respond. When you're walking out your life with patience,
people or circumstances do not dictate your words or actions
or your feelings of self-worth. Patience keeps you focused on
God and not on circumstances. This fruit is rooted in love
and solitude and does not waver in the storms of life. It's okay
with waiting because it knows God is always worth the wait. It
doesn't rush through half-open doors, as patience knows that
walking out of hiddenness in power is the goal. It is also active
in the waiting; it's in the word, it's in God's presence, and is
always ready to move, but not in an anxious way—in a super
chill, peaceful, loving, and joyful way.

BE ACTIVELY KIND

You can't feel lonely if your goal is kindness. Kindness isn't
something you only disperse to kind people; it's for all people. It's love's response to humanity and should be an active
response in your everyday life. If empathy and maturity had
a baby, it would be kindness. It's not just a reaction to people
doing nice things to you or for you; it's your response to all
people because you have encountered the love of God, and

you want others to as well. Loneliness cannot blur your vision while you're wearing kindness glasses, as kindness reminds our emotions to see people with empathy and coats our perspective on our quality of life and relationships with gratitude.

STAY ROOTED IN GOODNESS

You can't feel lonely if you've experienced God's goodness. Goodness is epic; it's like a superpower! It's what comes out of you when you've spent time in the presence of your creator. It keeps you from striving and getting burned out. When God created the world, he said, "It is good." Not "it is great." The power of the Holy Spirit activated in your life gives you the patience and insight into making things good, and seeing things as good so God can make things great. If you're striving for greatness all alone, loneliness will find you there; stay rooted in goodness. Good, not great, is always the goal.

FOCUS ON FAITHFULNESS

You can't feel lonely if you're walking in the shade of God's faithfulness. Faithfulness is strength in the face of adversity. Its foundation is the loyalty and steadfastness that keeps us loving people even when we are hurt or betrayed or left alone. And it keeps us shaded in heavenly solitude when isolation feels like an easier path. Faithfulness powered by the Holy Spirit combats loneliness and attacks to our feelings with the foundational facts we need to keep our focus on God.

God is always near to us (Psalm 145:18–19).

God will never leave us or forsake us (Deuteronomy 31:6).

God will help us and hold us up (Isaiah 41:10).

God is with us (Isaiah 43:2).

God guards our heart and mind (Philippians 4:7).

The fruit of faithfulness is a throat-puncher. And Jesus understood this fruit needed to be activated as he was going to head into tons of tough situations, the situations where the facts about his heavenly Father had to be louder and bigger than the crucifying moments in front of him.

GET TO KNOW GENTLENESS

You can't feel lonely if you've locked arms with gentleness. Gentleness is the ability to soften your words and your heart with grace, and it keeps us from screaming matches and road rage. It kept Jesus on the right path and focused on the right things when the Pharisees and the enemy wanted to pick fights with him. This fruit reminds us to respond with kindness and not allow what we feel today to ruin our tomorrow. Gentleness is underrated but so very important. It tells loneliness that yes, you may be by yourself, but you are never alone. And it doesn't do it in a way that it's offensive or intense, but one that is powered by love, joy, peace, patience, faithfulness, and gentleness.

SELF-CONTROL, GROW SOME

You can't feel lonely if your foundation is poured with self-control. Self-control isn't the ability to stop doing something whenever you want; it's the discipline of surrender to Jesus. It also looks like discretion, the art of knowing what you should be doing. This discretion and ability to pause and assess pushes us forward even when we feel alone in a crowded room. Self-control also keeps us tethered to the truth in God's presence and in God's word, through discernment. Discernment is the ability to know what God is doing in the room. And Jesus had both of these pillars cultivated by his discipline of surrender. It keeps us moving from tough life moments to solitude, solitude to a heavenly perspective, and back into the beautiful mess that is life and feelings. Self-control is cultivated in treks back to Nazareth and powered by the Holy Spirit. It's not an easy fruit to grow, but a fruit that will change your life if you take the time to grow it and activate it.

In a world where everyone seemed lonely, isolated, and rooted in some grand pursuit of the limelight, Jesus chose intentional hiddenness over and over again. He did this not only because he knew that moments of walking away and spending time alone with his heavenly Father would activate the Holy Spirit's fruit he needed, but also because healthy solitude would grow his ability to navigate loneliness's blinding effects. Just like in the time of Jesus, people are still lonely, isolated, and rooted in some grand pursuit of the limelight. Just jump on social media for two minutes, and you'll find the masses filling their hearts and minds with people, places, and things instead of solitude. I'm not judging, because I do this too all the time. It's worse for me, though, because I know the solution for the blurry vision loneliness throws at me, yet I still forget and add on things, knowing full well I already have everything I need!

But thank God for his goodness that sees past our short-comings and nudges us gently toward hiddenness: the intentional hiding away that matures us and the spirit-led moments that empower the healthy fruit and emotions cultivated in walks with his Spirit. When loneliness is triggered in your heart and mind and blurs your perspective on your quality of life and relationships, do as Jesus did.

Make solitude a priority.

Identify what triggers your loneliness.

Embrace hiddenness, even if its looks like Nazareth, and even if it looks like a wilderness.

Power up with the Holy Spirit.

Become a fruit basket.

Don't be fearful of the desert.

Onward.

CHAPTER 3

HIS WORD

How to deal with feeling afraid

Fear only thrives where love
does not abide.

don't like to be scared. I've always been confused by people who like to be afraid. I don't frequent Halloween horror nights; I don't watch scary movies; I don't do roller coasters. I do not find it fun or enjoyable to feel fear of any kind. Maybe it's because I live with a consistent batch of irrational fears about sharks, spiders, and potential excursions that

47

will lead to my life being told in some low-budget true crime documentary. Or maybe it's my mom and dad's fault for letting me watch *Jaws* and *Silence of the Lambs* as a kid. Or perhaps it's the fact that I live in Florida, where spiders will throw their babies at you. Maybe I can chalk it up to my childhood being filled to the brim with episodes of *Unsolved Mysteries* and *America's Most Wanted*, and images of white painter vans driven by weirdos in hipster glasses. In any case, I have always struggled with fear, the feeling caused by a belief that someone or something is going to come and cause me some kind of physical or emotional pain.

I do understand there is a healthy, primal fear that is innately built into all of us that keeps us from petting wild bears and sharks. And then, of course, there are rational fears tied to real-life things, like losing a child or death. I'm all good with primal fear, as I have no desire to pet something that could attack me or swim with something that could eat me. I'm also surprisingly levelheaded in very scary real-life rational circumstances. There was this one time my friend Katie—not her real name—and I were on a trip in Europe, and some super sketchy dudes jumped the fence behind us and began to follow us on the trail we were walking.

You should know I have thug tendencies, and when I realized we were being followed, I began to take off my hoop earrings and rings and calmly told Katie to prepare herself to run. I was totally prepared to fight these two dudes who looked like they starred in the movie *Taken*, opposite Liam Neeson. The truth is these potential kidnappers—or probably just two guys going for a walk—would have really been after Katie, as she is a total babe. I, on the flip side, am problematic and may or may not have turned around and walked aggressively at them with my hands spread out, screaming, "You gotta problem? Let's go!" They just awkwardly stared at me like two deer caught in headlights and immediately turned and walked away. Not sure if it was because of my thug persona that they got scared off, but that's not the point! The point is that you can be certain that if you are ever in a potential kidnapping, real-world rational fear situation, I will be semi-levelheaded, ready for a fight, and unafraid. Seriously, I've jumped out of a moving car as an adult to confront someone who hurt someone I care about. When it comes to protecting those I love from danger, I'm your girl. Spiders, sharks, and camping excursions? Not your girl!

Even though I navigate rational and primal fear like a champ, I struggle deeply in the realm of unhealthy irrational fear. Not because I struggle with phobias, but because when I'm faced with stressful circumstances that I perceive as harmful, I believe irrational lies about people, circumstances, and whatever I'm facing. And this kind of fear always wins when I'm exhausted emotionally and spiritually. It makes me an easy target when my heart and mind are focused on the lies fear fabricates instead of the love and truth of God. My fight with irrational fear always causes me to go from "everything is amazing, and Jesus has my back" to "the rapture happened, and I've been left behind" in .05 seconds. And the truth is that 100 percent of the time, fear lies to me about the situation and about the outcomes of whatever circumstance fear has found me in.

My worst bout with this fear happened at the age of thirty, when I found out I could not have kids. I know that a normal and rational response to infertility issues would look like grief, anger, or disappointment. And yes, I felt all of those emotions deeply, but it was the fear of the unknown, and loss of legacy, that I struggled through most. But before I jump into all that, let's give you some context.

Ya girl is what the Bible writers call barren. I loathe that word, by the way, as I don't subscribe to it. But I have spent a good portion of my adult life contending with "lady problems," and sadly, after a few years of not being able to get pregnant, I found out pregnancy would not be a possibility for the hubs and me. This was, of course, devastating. Even though I survived several emergency intestinal surgeries as a child where I had to be life-flighted, a major cancer scare at twenty-six, and a horrible car crash in my thirties, nothing, not one thing, filled me with the level of fear and dread about my future that infertility did.

Infertility caused me to reevaluate my entire life in a not-so-healthy way. The fear of it made me believe I was unloved by God and that I would be unloved by my husband and my family. It made me believe tons of false constructs, and it became all I knew, all I lived out, and all I followed. This fear told me my dreams of a family were now impossible and that my desire to be a mom was now worthless. It also filled my heart with the lie that I'd never leave a legacy and I'd leave this world with nothing. Everything was reexamined and evaluated while I was consumed with this fear.

In those initial months of learning about my infertility, fear and its lies caused me to run in the opposite direction of Jesus and the word of God. Ironically, I ran from the two things I needed desperately to stomp out my fear and distress. Sadly, I believed all the lies fear fed me, and I allowed fear to sow into my heart a wave of unhealthy anger toward God and whatever plans he had for me. See, Jesus knew full well that I had my baby names all picked out and that I'd always dreamed of being a mom to a little girl who would, unfortunately, inherit my cackle and a little boy who had my husband's eyes. I remember telling God that I was a good person who had the innate ability to love and mother and nurture and that I was created for motherhood.

And it was in that moment of despair, when I took my fear to God in an honest way, that I felt the Holy Spirit whisper, "Chari, infertility hasn't stolen your ability to be a mom; your fear has." Fear, the liar, had befallen me in those early months, and had now somehow convinced me that my hunger to love and experience love and nurture and reproduce good people who love Jesus had been stolen by infertility. But that was a total lie I would eventually uncover with being loved and choosing love as my response. Fear also talked me into believing that the God who had provided health and wholeness and safety throughout my many health issues as a child or lady problems as an adult had forgotten me somehow in this season. And to top it all off, fear and its lies had destroyed the way I saw myself and the way I perceived how the world saw me. I was overwhelmed, lonely, and full of fear.

DEAR JESUS, HELP

You know what you need when you're full of fear? Opinions. Everyone's thoughts and stories and views on your own personal fear zone.

Just kidding—that's the actual opposite of what you need. I'm not saying that you don't need to reach out for help if you're struggling; help is great, but a heavenly perspective of love is what you need more than you need people. When infertility popped up on the scene, everyone and their mama had a version of my story and felt compelled to tell me about it—in public, in private, via email, and via social media. It was like I was a target for help that I didn't want or ask for and help that focused on what the doctors said about me instead of who God said I was. There was also a slew of people who felt compelled to lay hands on my non-working womb. My actual worst nightmare. Do you know what I really needed facing fear and lies? To be loved and experience love. I needed Jesus and needed to hear directly from Jesus.

I needed Jesus, love personified, to speak to who I was and

not what fear was telling me or what the doctors said about me. I needed to hear how he navigated unmet expectations and lies, and attacks to his significance and perspective. What I needed was a crash course on how love navigated the feelings of fear and the lies it tries to build in our hearts and minds. Did Jesus run in the wrong direction like I did? Did he need people to speak into his life? Because they were coming out of the woodwork! What did Jesus do?

And what I discovered in my Gospel searches was that Jesus didn't run away from potentially frightening situations. I'd let fear become the loudest voice in my head, and Jesus's loudest voice was love. Jesus was love and knew love and didn't let any voice speak into who he was apart from that. Nope, when Jesus faced fear and lies, he met each scenario with love and compassion. This filter of love for the Father and his compassion for people dispelled any possible fear and lies, and any unsolicited advice that fed into the lies. It was love and love alone that launched him into his ministry days, and it was love and love alone that he leaned on in moments when fear tried to speak loudly over his life.

In Matthew 4, we find that Jesus gets sent into the wilderness by the Holy Spirit to be tempted by the enemy. We know from the last chapter that what Jesus cultivated in that wilderness were the power of the Holy Spirit and healthy emotions that would propel him forward. But that doesn't take away the fact that it was scary, and that Jesus had to navigate primal, rational, and irrational fears in the process. The story doesn't actually say Jesus was scared. But alone, in a wilderness, starving, dehydrated, depleted, and having a convo with Satan doesn't really sound like a good time. It sounds horrifying!

The last person who had a convo with the enemy ruined the world, and now Jesus was going to have to go navigate the same thing. When Jesus walked into the wilderness, fear and all its lies attacked what Jesus knew to be true. And fear did this by telling lies about Jesus's hunger, his significance, and his perspective: all things that were rooted in his heavenly Father's love. And what I noticed in my infertility journey was that fear attacked me in the same way by attacking what I knew to be true.

FILL UP ON THE SCRIPTURES

Fear cannot lie to you if you personally know the truth, and Jesus was and is the truth. Jesus gets baptized, and then the Holy Spirit leads him into the wilderness to be tempted. Jesus, knowing the Holy Spirit and His Father on the deepest of levels, says yes and heads on in there. At the end of these forty days and forty nights, the Bible says in the Voice translation, "After this fast, He was, as you can imagine, hungry. But He was also curiously stronger, when the tempter came to Jesus."

Note that Jesus was stronger even in the scary; he was stronger even when depleted and starving. Remember, the spirit *led* him into the wilderness and *through* the wilderness. He came out of the wilderness in the *power* of the Holy Spirit. Whatever you are facing, God is with you! This means that even if what you are facing is legit scary, you are not alone; God is going to see you through, and you are going to be stronger at the end of whatever it is. And that makes everything less scary!

Then we see that the devil points out that Jesus is hungry, which is super passive-aggressive, because fear is sneaky and comes at you with half-truths that keep your focus on the problem instead of God. "If You are the Son of God, tell these stones to become bread." What I discovered in reading the Matthew 4 account of the wilderness is that when life depletes you emotionally and spiritually, fear and its lies are just around the corner to attack our hunger first. For Jesus, it was physical hunger, and it was the wilderness trek that depleted him. For me, my hunger was my desire for legacy, and it was the diagnosis of infertility that depleted me and filled me with fear.

Jesus responded with strength found in the love he'd experienced with his heavenly Father and the love produced in him by the Holy Spirit. Another way of looking at this response is he responded with authority found in the Holy Spirit and clarity found in the scriptures: "Man does not live by bread alone. Rather, he lives on every word that comes from the mouth of the Eternal One." Jesus wasn't just regurgitating a revelation about the scriptures; he was quoting actual scripture, actual bread he lived on found in Deuteronomy 8:3. In my bout with fear, I responded by running in every direction but to Jesus and the scriptures. It's like the lies about my situation trumped

God's love for me and the plans and purposes I knew he had in place for me. If you find yourself hungry, living off lies, and starving for a lost dream stolen by fear, ask yourself, am I not already full on the word of God?

Am I not already fully loved and seen by the Father?

Am I not focused on the purposes and call to love God and love his people?

Isn't God enough?

Do you know God?

Like, do you really know him and what he believes about you?

When we walk out of bouts of fear with a deep understanding of who God is and who God says we are, our emotions fall under that shade of how loved and cherished we are. And fear and lies cannot thrive where love abides. Jesus was living in love because he knew love. And that call to love and the mission that would inevitably bring freedom to humanity was larger than his hunger at that moment, and it made me wonder, was my hunger for legacy and motherhood that opened the door to fear larger than my desire to see God glorified through my brokenness?

Fear told me my hunger was bigger and better and more important than anything else. It also told me that God couldn't use me if this hunger wasn't satisfied, specifically with children of my own. My response to fear was "Really? Oh my God, my life is now over! Tell me more."

Jesus told fear that there was nothing more important than

the Father and his plans to see his creation walking in total freedom and wholeness. And so, based on Jesus's words and his response to the attack on his hunger, I surrendered hunger for children of my own, I relinquished my fear of being unable to leave a legacy, and I chose to live out love instead. I may not be able to have kids of my own to love, but I can love my neighbor. I can love my husband. I can love my parents and my siblings. I can love the stranger in the supermarket and the guy who cuts me off in traffic. I can love you. All people that I've attached to the legacy of love.

When love became my focus, I stopped filling up my mind and heart with reruns of *Grey's Anatomy* and *How I Met Your Mother*, and I dove into the scriptures and watched messages about living a fruitful life instead. What you ingest matters, especially when you're navigating fear's lies. I then started vocalizing God's word about my brokenness. I stopped saying things like "I'm infertile," or that I was "battling infertility" when people asked me why I couldn't have kids. My responses shifted toward how fruitful my life was instead of the fruit I wasn't producing.

I then stopped taking in unsolicited advice, and I surrounded myself with life-giving people who spoke to the truth of God's word about me, and not the lies fear was saying about me. I don't know what lies fear has told you, and I don't know what you are feeding on daily to combat those lies. But I'll tell you this: I love a good day on the couch watching Netflix. But if you are navigating fear that lies to you, you're going to need to go read your Bible to remind yourself how big God is and how loved you are by God. Also, one glass of wine is enough, and call that friend back who keeps asking you out for coffee. Nothing will be able to drown out the lies except Jesus and understanding how loved you are. Fear thrives in darkness; you're going to need to get into the light of the word and actual life-giving people to navigate unhealthy irrational fear.

Also, what are you hungry for? Success, a relationship, a job, kids? Whatever it is, the enemy will come for it. So make sure your desire for Jesus and his plan and purpose to be love, and produce love, is growing in place of fear. Because if you don't, you're going to live an unsatisfied, hungry life, one that feeds on counterfeit love, acceptance, and significance. Jesus looked at the enemy in complete exhaustion and still responded with truth and love found in scripture in a scary circumstance where lies were trying to take root. When you fill up on the scriptures, you meet love. The love that sent his Son to die a horrible death on a cross to redeem our sins. The love that fights off fear and that never leaves you alone. The kind of love Jesus tapped into when he overcame Gethsemane and trekked back to Nazareth for more hiddenness. The kind of love that said yes to forty days and nights in the wilderness. When you experience that kind of love found in the scriptures, found in a relationship with God, God then helps you redefine your dreams and desires to combat fear and its lies.

KNOW AND UNDERSTAND
THE SCRIPTURES

Fear cannot lead you with its lies if you are guided by love. The second thing fear attacked in Jesus's wilderness story was significance. Jesus is exhausted and hungry and is taken to the highest place in Jerusalem and taunted: "If You are the Son of God, jump! And then we will see if You fulfill the Scripture that says, 'He will command His heavenly messengers concerning You, and the messengers will buoy You in their hands so that You will not crash, or fall, or even graze Your foot on a stone'" (Matthew 4:6 VOICE). Jesus is face-to-face with the enemy, the author of fear and lies, the orchestrator of all doubt and confusion whose sole purpose is to steal, kill, and destroy your perspective and dreams, and yet Jesus responds like a total gangster. The Voice translation of the Matthew 4 story says Jesus responded, "That is not the only thing Scripture says, It also says, 'Do not put the Eternal One, your God, to the test.'"

Jesus, in that moment, facing fear with absolute exhaustion and depletion, was still motivated by love for his Father and the people he would eventually give his life for, still responded with his significance intact and with total authority. The enemy used scripture to try to trick Jesus into believing the lies he was tossing at him, yet Jesus, the Son of God, the Messiah, was not going to be tripped up by fear spitting out broken and corrupt interpretations of scripture at him. John 1:1–4 describes Jesus as the word: "In the beginning was the Word, and the

Word was with God, and the Word was God. He was in the beginning with God. All things were made through him, and without him was not any thing made that was made. In him was life, and the life was the light of men. The light shines in the darkness, and the darkness has not overcome it" (ESV).

Jesus was the word made flesh, and his identity and significance were rooted in love long before this moment in the wilderness came to fruition. His significance saw creation unfold and man be formed from dust. His significance didn't let fear and lies tell him he wasn't really the Son of God as he knew he was the Lamb seated on the throne, the King of Kings and Lord of Lords. He witnessed "Let there be light," and light has not stopped. He was going to be the healer of the sick, lame, and blind. Jesus knew he was on the earth to steal the keys back from death and the one called to redeem humanity from Eve's mistake in the garden. Jesus, even in his depleted and hungry state, would not be shaken by polluted scriptures, because he was the scripture; he knew the scripture, as it was the bread he lived on. I, on the other hand, totally believed the broken and corrupt interpretations of scripture that fear threw at me.

I believed the lie fear threw at me that the mandate to be fruitful and multiply found in Genesis 1 had removed me from the blessings and covering of God. I believed my failure to produce in the flesh stopped me from producing anything substantial for the Kingdom. Truth is, my perspective was so shattered by fear that I needed Jesus to come in with love, explain what I couldn't see, and tell fear to leave, as I didn't have the words to fight it off. I needed Jesus, the word of God, to walk into the room and tell fear, "You don't want this smoke; back off! I am love, and I know love, and this one is loved by me!" I needed love to tell me the truth in the sea of lies I was drowning in. I needed love to remind me,

> **I am not broken:** "I am fearfully and wonderfully made" (Psalm 139:14).
>
> **I am not barren:** "Because more are the children of the desolate woman than of her who has a husband" (Isaiah 54:1).
>
> **I will have a legacy:** "For I know the plans I have for you," declares the Lord, "plans to prosper you and not to harm you, plans to give you hope and a future" (Jeremiah 29:11).
>
> **I have no need to fear:** "The Lord is my light and my salvation—whom shall I fear? The Lord is the stronghold of my life—of whom shall I be afraid?" (Psalm 27:1).
>
> **I have no need to worry:** "Do not be anxious about anything, but in every situation, by prayer and petition, with thanksgiving, present your requests to God. And the peace of God, which transcends all understanding, will guard your hearts and your minds in Christ Jesus" (Philippians 4:6–7).
>
> **I am not alone:** "He found him in a desert land, and

in the howling waste of the wilderness; he encircled him, he cared for him, and he kept him as the apple of his eye" (Deuteronomy 32:10).

What verses do you go to when fear tells you you're not enough? What verses do you run to when fear reminds you of your failures? If you guard your life and your thoughts with the scriptures in moments where fear is running amok, the lies fear throws your way will fall on deaf ears and a heart that is already overflowing with a firm identity. Real talk—fear, and its lies, will attack your hunger and significance if you are not filling up on the word of God and living your life through the filter of the word of God. It's only in God's word that you will be strengthened with a firm identity. The word, Jesus, knows who you are, what you are purposed for, and only he can cause fear to vanish in an instant.

I said a few paragraphs up that Jesus navigated fear by the love of his heavenly Father and Jesus's love for people. And so this is where I tell you that you are so loved by the Father that he has me navigating my crazy emotions and writing these pages just to remind you that fear has no place where love resides. God has called you to more than what you realize, and you don't need to be afraid, for he is with you, and it's his truth about you that matters, that creates a legacy, and that impacts eternity.

I know some of you out there are saying to yourselves, "Chari, are you saying when I'm full of fear, the only fix is reading the Bible? That sounds too easy and a bit lame!" But what if I'm right? What if you lived out this temporal life and navigated fear with love and love birthed in eternity as your guide? What if love and spending time with love was your first response to unhealthy emotions? And just in case you missed it, when I say love, I mean Jesus and his word. Jesus chose love in his life, in his responses, and as a result, Jesus modeled healthy emotions. I believe we can do the same if we choose to know love, live out love, and finally truly follow love with all we are, even when we are scared, even when fear is spitting out lies.

STAY IN THE SCRIPTURES

Fear cannot befriend you with its lies if you are pursuing love. In Matthew 4:8–10, Jesus and the enemy are still going at it in the wilderness after forty days and nights of testing, and now the enemy is asking Jesus to worship him. He takes Jesus to the top of a mountain, and he shows Jesus all the kingdoms of the world and all their awesomeness and then begins this convo:

Devil: If You bow down and worship me, I will give You all these kingdoms.

Jesus: Get away from Me, Satan. I will not serve you. I will instead follow Scripture, which tells us to "worship the Eternal One, your God, and serve only Him" (VOICE).

When faced with fear, I tend to have convos with fear, kind of like Eve in the garden. Fear and its lies hit pause on my following, and then fear steals my ability to see God as bigger than whatever is causing me fear. But Jesus models here in the wilderness that convos with fear and its lies are not a thing. The only words you ever need to tell fear are "Get away from me." I will say it loud sometimes for good measure. I will remind fear whom I serve and place God at the forefront of my moment, as Jesus did. The enemy knows that if he gets fear's lies to befriend your expectations, significance, and perspective, you will worship whatever he throws in front of you to satisfy those desires. For me, that meant whatever was going to give me children, from IVF treatments to adoption. I was ready and waiting to toss my hunger for motherhood and the significance and perspective I thought I'd find in motherhood at the feet of fear if it would give me what I wanted.

Just in case there is someone reading this who thinks I settled or that I view my hunger for motherhood as potentially bad—I did not settle, and my desire to love and be loved and to expound upon that love through others has always been the desire of my heart. Motherhood on this side of eternity may look like children, but motherhood, parenthood, in the kingdom is so much more. It's a God mandate for you and for me to be walking vessels of God's love in the world. And it's something I have dedicated my life to producing and cultivating, whether in moments where all is well or in moments where I or others are overcome with fear's lies about me.

But fear corrupted that desire and hunger to love and be love and made it something bigger than my love for God and his purposes. And when I allowed that hunger, motivated by fear, to be my guide, I lost my identity in God and the perspective that God was enough. Yet it was and is only God who builds legacies and fulfills dreams, and it would only be God who could make my life matter beyond my years, not my ability to produce children. I just had to shift my cravings for legacy and motherhood to love found in God's word, his plans, and his ways, as those three essential things hold the key to our hunger, significance, and our perspective. Those three things will beat out fear and unhealthy feelings that infiltrate our hearts and minds every single time! Though my hunger was for legacy and motherhood, love has always been the goal. Though I thought my significance would only be manifested with children, love for God's people filled that gap. Though I perceived children as the only way to leave a legacy, love showed me how to truly build a legacy by just loving those I encounter daily.

What have you thrown at the feet of fear in hopes that it would go away? What have you hungered for that you haven't realized or that perhaps has meant more to you than walking out of that wilderness fear-free? I'm not talking spiders or heights; I'm talking maybe you jumped into a relationship too fast because you were scared you'd be alone or single forever. I'm talking about taking a job you knew would take you away from your kids and family because your hunger for success drove you. I don't know what your hunger is, but we all have one. No judgment; we all have to work through the temporal hunger that fear loves to attack. But if you can't recognize what you're hungry for, an attack on your significance and perspective will be coming next if it hasn't already been hit by fear. So take a moment, pause from the book if you have to, and get alone with God and ask him to reveal it to you. Whatever it is, surrendering your hunger at the feet of God isn't a weird thing. It's just being able to say "God, I have this hunger, and I love this (insert your hunger here). But I love you more and I want to hand it over to you, so you can make all the good I have great, and focused on love."

My fear master class led me through the wilderness of infertility, and though it was a less than ideal journey, I am thankful for the trek. It took my unmet expectations and hunger and shifted my appetites toward love, toward being love and producing love. The trek also gave me a mirror of the life of Jesus and how significance and perspective can only be found in the mirror of the Father, as God the Father doesn't have convos with fear; God the Father is motivated by love. Your fear master class may be linked to being single or your desire to get married. Maybe it's having a bustling career or a relationship with family or friends restored. Or maybe it's attached to being a good parent or, in my case, not being a parent. But whatever your fear is attached to, don't listen to its lies. And if you feel like perhaps you may be lost in the lies of fear, fill up on the truth about you, and your feelings found only in God's word, as it's God's truth that fear's lies cannot shake.

His bread is enough to fill your hunger.

His words are enough for you to find your significance.

His love is enough to shift your perspective.

Focus on love, love found and experienced in the scriptures.

Love is always the answer.

God is with you.

Onward.

CHAPTER 4

HIS WAYS

How to deal with feeling unsafe

Safety is found in the pursuit of Jesus.

I live in Florida, which my Australian friend calls the Australia of the United States. We have been known to have small dinosaurs called alligators strolling across our golf courses and sunbathing in our pools, water moccasins that will slither after you for no reason, and wolf spiders that rise up at you as if you owe them money. Let's not forget the palmetto bugs—or, as the rest of the world calls them, giant roaches that fly. We also have aggressive bull sharks in our rivers, non-indigenous pythons and boa constrictors in our Everglades, and hurricanes; let's not forget the hurricanes. And just for good measure, I live in the area that is considered the lightning capital of North America. So if the mosquitoes and humidity don't get you, the lightning possibly could. Don't get me wrong, I love where I live, and I've lived in Florida most of my life, but feeling unsafe and exposed to potential dangers kind of goes with the territory.

In Florida, we combat these dangers with screens. We have screens for everything because everything wants to bite you or set up shop in your house. Screens around the pools, screens around the porches, screens on the windows and on the doors. It's like Oprah showed up and is out here giving out free screens. But I won't lie; I'm thankful for the screens in Florida, and also for the screens in my life that give me a sense of comfort and a feeling of safety, as life and people feel like Florida to me most days. By that I mean it's like everything and everyone is out to pick a fight or ransack my day with its suffocating humidity. In response, I've had to screen my life meticulously and consistently with a healthy community, peace, and firm boundaries; a community that follows Jesus and that I have to sow time and energy into; a peace that only comes from spending time with Jesus, and hefty boundaries that keep my emotional reservoir filled with love. Community, peace, and healthy boundaries are the cheat sheets to feeling safe and safeguarding your emotions. But that wasn't something I understood early on in my adulthood. I just blindly walked through life, hoping for the best. I assumed community was the crowd I frequented, peace was a feeling that came and went based on my circumstance, and boundaries were not even on my radar. I lived my life like this for years, hoping for the best and consistently feeling unsafe in my emotions, my words, and my actions. I longed for the type of community that would keep me accountable, model peace and boundaries, and help me feel safe. But I wasn't very good at pursuing people or Jesus enough to set the right screens or safeguards in place.

The breaking point—or my *aha* moment, if you want to be positive about it—that uncovered my extreme need for these three screens happened after my sunshine of a husband and I bought an old house one year and eight months into our marriage. I will now, and for the rest of this chapter, lovingly refer to this home as the Little Shop of Horrors. The LSOH was what the kids nowadays call a fixer-upper, something those people on those DIY home design shows could have made beautiful in two weeks. But we bought the home not to fix it up but because it was the only house in the area we could afford. The area was scary, but it was super central to our families and our jobs. The house was historic and built in 1929, but we figured if it had survived that long it should be all right.

And by "all right," I mean after we moved in, we found there were no screens, no central A/C, no insulation, and a colony of raccoons and rats battling it out to live in the attic and have total domination of our ducts and vents. The floor was caving in, and because it had been vacant for so long the neighborhood vagrants were using it as a drug house in the summer and a warm place to sleep in the winter. Did I mention yet that the city had accidentally paved the road in such a way that when it rained, the water flooded our front and back yards? I will now go cry in a corner at the thought that I bought and lived in this home. So there's that.

Back to the story. So it was now ours, and we began the essential and minimal renovations that would allow us to live there with some kind of safety and comfort. We painted, we fixed the floors, we painted a bit more, and then my husband fell through the floor. We fixed the floor again. We got into midnight fights with the wolf spiders, rats, and raccoons. And to add a little icing on this Little Shop of Horrors cake, we were robbed three different times in the first month that we lived there. First, they took everything on our front porch. The second time, they took everything off our back porch; then the third time, they tried to break into the house when we were not there. I felt unsafe in every single way. I had no peace, and the home that should have been a safe boundary for my rest and life was being invaded by people who wanted to do illicit drugs in my makeshift kitchen! My husband went into safety mode and sent me to buy a dog that was large and menacing while he went out to get a security company to come and install a security system into our LSOH that very day. By the time I got home with the puppies, the security system was in place and ready to go.

Notice I said puppies? He sent me to buy a dog that was intimidating and would scare people, and instead, I brought home two beautiful tiny puppies that fit into my hand and that we could not afford. Please note that I was really good at making bad life decisions back then. Thankfully, my husband did not make decisions based on feelings or the cuteness of puppies we did not need or could not afford; his decisions were based on our safety. That night, we went to bed with Rocco and Salvatore, our two pit bull/rottweiler–looking puppies; our cat, Gato Gordo; and the clan of rats and raccoons in the attic. I again hoped for the best!

Around three a.m., vagrants wanting to use my kitchen came knocking and kicked the back door wide open. The alarm immediately sounded. In my sleepy stupor, I gently moved the puppies, kicked the cat off the bed, walked over to the alarm system, and put the code in to stop the alarm. Once the alarm stopped, I said, "I got it" to my husband and crawled back into bed to go back to sleep. What I had forgotten was that turning off the alarm would also stop the alarm people from checking on us and the police from coming to help. My husband, standing there in shock, screamed, "Why would you do that?!" Thankfully, the alarm scared these guys away, but it didn't make us feel any safer, and it showed my husband that I have a proclivity for making bad life decisions, especially when it came to our family being exposed to dangerous situations.

Have you ever lived a life like this? Frequenting potentially hostile people, circumstances, or environments with no screens in place, no alarms set, and surrounded by the wrong safeguards?

How about this: Have you ever been to a party that you knew would get you in trouble? Ever dated anyone whose values didn't align with yours, and a few months into it, you didn't recognize yourself? Exposing yourself to danger or schemes of the enemy may sound convoluted or antiquated for some, but it's a real thing we do on a daily basis. And we do it without realizing that exposing ourselves to danger feeds unhealthy emotions within us, emotions like loneliness and fear, frustration, and helplessness. These are all emotions fastened tightly to feeling unsafe. And even though we know this, we still venture out without screens. We do it because culture says biblical boundaries are old school, true community is found online, and following Jesus is for the religious. So in moments where my bad life decisions are exposing me to danger and the schemes of the enemy, I look at the life of Jesus, the life that walked out of the wilderness with power, and I follow his ways accordingly.

SAFETY IS FOUND IN COMMUNITY

In Matthew 3, we find Jesus out of the wilderness, full of the Holy Spirit. Now he begins to build his crew, what would become his community. Why, you may wonder? Well, because his cousin, John the Baptist, has been put in prison. John the Baptist had been preaching about the coming King of the Jews and picking fights with the religious elite and those in power along the way. The Romans did not like any kind of uprising or movement that would take glory from Caesar, so they didn't love it when he said that Jesus was the coming Messiah, or when he questioned their very wicked and perverse lifestyles. And now the guy who'd just baptized Jesus had been arrested for calling out Herod Antipas's marriage to his wife, Herodias, as illegal, because she had previously been married to Herod's brother, Philip. In a nutshell, those speaking and living contrary to the Roman occupation at the time were always exposing themselves to danger just by breathing. Jesus was living in dangerous, unsafe times, and so right after he finds out about John, the Bible tells us, "Now when Jesus heard John had been put in prison, he departed to Galilee" (Matthew 3:12 NKJV).

Jesus is saddened and has every reason to feel unsafe. And so he withdraws to a city by the sea, where he invites a few young fishermen into community: the community that would one day change the entire world! "As Jesus was walking beside the Sea of Galilee, he saw two brothers, Simon called Peter and his brother Andrew. They were casting a net into the lake, for they were fishermen. 'Come, follow me,' Jesus said, 'and I will send you out to fish for people.' At once they left their nets and followed him" (Matthew 4:18–20).

Also, I think it's important to note that Jesus was Jewish,

and living in a thriving community was very much part of his culture, a culture rooted in a deep understanding of covenant, commitment, and loyalty. And so we find that after they are called to join Jesus's crew these guys drop their nets—their nets, the thing that gave them identity and that attached them to their family's legacy. Jesus wasn't looking for followers on social who needed a platform or carried their nets while following Jesus. He was looking for brothers and sisters, people who would drop their nets and follow. His friendships looked different than what we'd call friends, and as a result, his community would become part of a kingdom legacy.

The community he sought would be made up of those he could trust to lock arms with in ministry and in life, as Jesus knew safety from the enemy's schemes, safety from the world's nonsense could easily be navigated in the safety of a strong community, the type of safe community that embraced his heavenly Father's mission with him and who weren't dragging their nets behind them. Nowadays, we deem safe friendship as the people whom we can just unleash our emotional grenades on, at all hours with no pushback. We view safe people as the crew whom we just talk smack about other people with. But that's a toxic community, not a safe community. Not a community on a mission that finds safety together from the enemy's lies and convos.

Also, I am well aware that these friends would eventually abandon and betray Jesus. These friends he treated like brothers. But Jesus showed us how to pick our friends. He picked a crew that could love well, who would be down for a difficult journey through deserts and storms. He chose friends who were humble and teachable and who had the strength to make a comeback! Every one of them, even Judas, tried to make a comeback after they famously betrayed Jesus in Matthew 26. You don't need people in your community who will never fail you; you need people in your community who will love you enough to say sorry, learn from their mistakes, and move forward.

What does your friend group look like? What does your community, the people you'd trust with your prized possessions, a key to your house, your pet, your kids, and your life, look like? I'm not talking about that random work best friend or the people you brunch with or those who follow you on social media. I'm talking about the friends who can show up at your house when it's not clean, and you are okay with that. Friends you can disagree with, and at the end of the night you hug, say I love you, and remain friends. Those people. Who are they? Write their name in the spaces on this page, as I'm sure they are already written on your life. Those people are the ones Jesus was looking for.

I love this type of friends, the ones that push you forward. The kind of friends who sharpen one another. These types of relationships don't come easy. They have to be searched out and fought for. Jesus understood that building a safe and strong community was an active pursuit. A safe community utilizes the power of the Holy Spirit to know who to build with, struggle with, laugh with, and do life with. The type of friends who will lovingly follow you into the garden, as you sweat blood when you are overwhelmed. The type of friends that when you are gone will speak of your legacy to the ends of the earth.

It's also important to look at where you're finding your community. Jesus found his community on the shores of Galilee, hustling! The first four guys he chose were young brothers who were fishermen. Simon, who would eventually be called Peter; Andrew; and the sons of Zebedee, James and John. These weren't like the cool young fishermen you see on social media with their coral-colored Salt Life sun shirts and Oakley sunglasses taking pictures with their caught fish. These guys were tough. They'd seen storms and had gone hungry, and they knew how to navigate struggle—exactly what Jesus needed. If you have the time to dive into Matthew 4, you'll see that Jesus is handpicking his circle, the guys he'd one day leave everything to, the guys who'd get a close-up view of his life and ministry. And the first few he chose were unlikely, unqualified, and what many would deem unfit for ministry work. Yet that's who he chose first! He didn't pick who the world would perceive as the best for the job. They were not the most studied; they weren't influencers, and they didn't have a following. But they could be trusted to follow, and that is what he needed when things were going to get hard.

Jesus dealt with the feeling of being unsafe and exposed to danger by making sure he was surrounded not only by his

Father's voice and the Holy Spirit's power, but by true friends. Did Jesus need a crew? I mean, if he was walking the earth in his heavenly body, with an army of angels, probably not. But he chose to walk the earth like us, flesh and blood and feelings, in need of community and safety, just like us. Jesus stepped out of the wilderness fight, and he instantly modeled the principle of living and building a community for us. Because he'd just got into it with the enemy, his friend had been imprisoned. He knew we would need boundaries and people around us to keep an eagle eye out for the attacks of the enemy. If you want to feel safe, surround yourself with a healthy community following Jesus. The type that speaks life and that sharpens you even when it hurts and even when you didn't ask for it. The type of community that is saturated with empathy. Those people—find them, pursue them, and hold on to them.

SAFETY IS FOUND IN PEACE, THE PERSON

In Matthew 4:21–22, Jesus has already gained two new friends, Simon and Andrew. He then walks up to James and John, getting their nets ready to go fishing. Again, guys who understand the importance of legacy, covenant, and dropping their nets. Jesus was a values guy, and it was important that those whom he was on mission with, or those who were to become intricate parts of his community, were bought into his values. He calls them over and gives them the same exact "follow me" call he gave Simon and Andrew, and it says in the Bible that they immediately *left the boat* they were in and *left their father* and followed Jesus. They left what would give them provision and what would leave them an earthly legacy to follow the provider, so they could make an eternal impact. Sometimes what you think is making you feel safe is like the puppies in my Little Shop of Horrors scenario. It's something you are hoping will one day grow into safety, but is not safe. I believe they gave up what looked safe and secure to follow Jesus into the unknown because they encountered peace. A peace that surpassed their understanding, and that peace was Jesus.

If you want to feel safe, then you have to have a healthy community. And right smack dab in the middle of that community, leading the way through storms and trials, has to be peace. Jesus, the Prince of Peace, is walking safety. There are no unsafe feelings when you're screened in by peace. And Jesus experienced this because he was attached to the Father and walking in the power of the Holy Spirit. So peace was like his thing! If you want to live and walk in peace, the type of peace that faced the garden, hiddenness, and the wilderness, you have to be attached to peace.

Peace is the person, not the feeling. There is no peace as a feeling apart from peace that is the person, and that person is Jesus Christ. If you want to feel safe, follow Jesus closely, intentionally, and alongside a strong community. If you are feeling unsafe, attacked by the enemy on all sides, and hoping for the best in your own LSOH, you probably aren't following Jesus closely enough. When you follow Jesus closely and intentionally, it will look like you're dropping your nets, leaving the boat, and tying your legacy to Jesus. It means dropping and leaving the things you use as identifiers apart from Jesus behind on the shore. As a result, Jesus becomes your filter.

Think about it like a bio: instead of putting what you do or what you are all about, you leave your bio blank and live a life that expresses the ways and truth of Jesus, the Prince of Peace. It's not words; it's actions. It's not a religious belief system; it's love in motion. We live in a time of influencers and platforms. And so did Jesus. What would it look like if we chose to influence those toward safety and peace and a life-giving community found in following Jesus? What would life look like if we used our platforms to express the love we experienced when we encountered the Prince of Peace? Life would look safe—safe enough for hurting people to be drawn in. And safe enough for those shunned by religion to finally be seen and valued.

When people find out I'm a pastor, they usually are shocked. I guess I don't really give off what they deem to be a pastor vibe. Non-religious people, people who aren't found in Sunday pews, usually seem relieved. Religious people tend to respond with questions about my schooling, or my preaching, or my political stance. And my answer is always the same to everyone: I have no desire to pick up nets that make other people comfortable. I just want to follow Jesus closely and love people well. As that's how Jesus and his disciples lived and responded and found safety. The Prince of Peace, who had healthy emotions in the midst of a dangerous world and who was daily attacked by the enemy, was a beacon of peace, a peace that signaled to those who felt unsafe and led the masses toward protection found in his community and his presence.

Someone just said to themself, "Chari, we are in chapter four; we are all following Jesus!" Are we? Or are we half asleep, turning off alarms? Most of us feel unsafe or attacked by the schemes of the enemy because our community is made up of puppies, no screens, mosquitoes, iPhones, and a social media following. I mean this metaphorically and kind of literally! We are unsafe, and we feel unsafe because we aren't following Jesus the way the disciples did and the way that impacts and loves people.

When the disciples said yes to Jesus, they dropped their nets and everything changed. They didn't just drop the things that were comfortable, convenient, or that fit with their personal truth, but they dropped everything! Following the Prince of Peace should change your words, your values, your emotions, and your belief system. In my early days of walking with Jesus closely, my unhealthy emotions were still guiding my words and my actions and reactions. And when people would get hurt or offended by something I said or did, my response was always that I was Cuban, and that Cubans are loud and passionate and they shouldn't feel offended. I did this for a hot minute until finally, a close friend pulled me aside and kindly said, "Chari, you gotta stop saying that as you are a follower of Jesus first before anything else. Your words and actions should respond as such."

Following the Prince of Peace should leave you without a net. And what people see in your life should be his net. I learned this over years of embarrassing myself in public and in front of friends and co-workers. If you say you believe in Jesus, but your actions in public and in private don't show it, then you are a bystander and not a follower. I know that's harsh, but so is a life following far behind and missing out on the safety and peace found in following closely. And I don't want you to embarrass yourself. Consider this me taking you aside like my friend did to me.

If you want to feel safe and really be protected from the schemes of the enemy, you have to actually get under the covering that walking the path of peace gives us: a covering that keeps us in community, a covering that helps navigate our emotions when the schemes of the enemy are all around us, and the kind of coverage that helps build a godly legacy. Legacies aren't built; they're left. And the only thing I want to leave behind at the end of my days is a life well lived for the cause of Christ and a community impacted by the love of Jesus. Because that's what Jesus left for us, a trail of love, and how to love and be love and produce those who love in return.

SAFETY IS FOUND IN
FIRM BOUNDARIES

The disciples left everything to follow Jesus and become part of Jesus's community. They also walked with peace because he was peace, and that is my hope and prayer for us, that when we are following Jesus and surrounded by good people, the screens will go up all around us and protect us from attacks that may cause us to stray from the safety found along the path of peace. Jesus goes on to end Matthew 4 by spreading the Gospel in various cities and healing sick people everywhere. He was strategic in his travel and in whom he surrounded himself with, but he was always abundant in his love. It says in verse 24 that even though he was traveling all over, "he healed them all" (VOICE). And that was very dangerous.

Jesus was on the earth to restore God's earthly family to its heavenly community. When Eve sinned, it caused a massive divide between heaven's initial plan for humanity and what humanity had become. Jesus, the Son of God, came to fill that divide with love and peace, and salvation. And he wasn't going to be detoured by anyone's opinions or belief systems about how he was meant to live out his heavenly Father's mission.

Even if it meant he would have to walk it all out among the religious elite of the time and the Roman occupation that would eventually lead to his execution.

The religious elite saw what Jesus was doing as a polluted version of what they hoped the Messiah would be. They believed the Messiah to be more of a military voice that would rescue them from the Roman occupation—not some hippie from a poor town with a sketchy birth story, surrounded by youth healing the sick. And the Romans were just merciless overlords who killed anyone and everyone who spoke against Caesar. Everything about Jesus's life and ministry was unsafe, yet he built a thriving community, walked in peace, and had very clear boundaries.

Jesus's clear boundaries surrounding his time looked like a hefty prayer life that engaged his heavenly Father, even if it was in the middle of the night and everyone was falling asleep. His time was ticking around the Holy Spirit, which meant Jesus's desire for closeness to his Father's voice was non-negotiable, a line he would not let anyone shift or speak into. Jesus also had no qualms about leaving his crew and circumstances to be alone with his Father and power up on the Holy Spirit. Having healthy emotions wasn't something he hoped for, but he fought for them, with clear boundaries surrounding his time. Time was intentionally set aside and guarded for prayer and solitude. And regardless of how weird he looked just disappearing into the deserts and gardens, he was going to do it without worry or concern for what others thought about his healthy hiddenness. He knew the Holy Spirit would help him navigate all the people he was encountering and the feelings associated with all those people.

To feel safe, you need community, peace, and boundaries: the type of boundaries that are positioned in your life with strategy and intentionality to keep you on the path of peace. What is the strategy in your life that keeps your boundaries in place to follow Jesus well? Where do you place your screens to keep your heart and mind safe and focused on Jesus? Jesus's life goal was to go to the lost and broken and those in need and bring freedom. And the strategy to walk that out was always the same—follow the father, love abundantly, do it all in community, repeat. This strategy kept Jesus from being bullied into situations he wasn't called to or meant for. It kept him out of arguments and unoffended by the religious. It kept him focused on solitude and rest when life got busy.

If our goal as followers of the Prince of Peace is the same, shouldn't we have a similar strategy and boundaries as well? Jesus's time on this earth was running out, so he made sure he was cultivating heaven's purposes with an earthly strategy. We, like Jesus, are not promised longevity, and the Bible describes this temporal life as a vapor. Don't waste your time; don't follow far behind; get close and put a strategy together to keep you on the path of peace.

What is your strategy for keeping your time and focus on God's plans and purpose for your life? What have you had to put boundaries around to keep you following Jesus closely?

Maybe you don't have one. And if you don't, that's okay! Let's make one today. Write it in a journal or on the edges of these pages, and I'll give you mine to help you spark boundaries that may help you.

The screens and boundaries in my life that keep me safe and that keep me following the path of peace, connected to a community, and focused on being love look like being strategic in:

- who I give my time to
- what I give my time to
- how much time I spend reading the word
- having date nights with my husband
- making the Sabbath a priority
- making Sunday church a priority
- going outside to just watch the sunset
- not watching movies or TV shows that don't speak to my values
- finding deliberate moments to laugh
- taking breaks from social media
- being intentional with my friendships
- FaceTiming with family over random text updates
- keeping a healthy work-life balance

These things may sound mundane, but they keep my mind and heart focused on the people and values that matter the most to me, which are following Jesus closely, loving my family intentionally, and embracing my community wholly. And if I'm a good steward of those things, I won't get overwhelmed or lonely, I won't be overcome by the lies of fear, and I will find safety along the path of peace.

Jesus did not stray from the moments and the people that really mattered. His time was guarded. His values were intact, and his road was set. The Gospel stories say that sometimes he only hung out with three friends, and sometimes he was surrounded by thousands. He knew when to engage in verbal tussles and when to walk away. There were moments, like in John 5 at the pool of Bethesda, when he walked into a situation full of sick people and only healed one guy! Jesus wasn't motivated by want or pressured by people's expectations of him; he was motivated by his purpose to see heaven and earth restored through love. And that love was safely guarded by the voice of his Father, the power of the Holy Spirit, a safe community, and clear boundaries that kept him moving along the path of peace.

In the life of Jesus, safety looked like living life in a community he pursued and mentored and encouraged. Safety looked like walking the path of peace and embracing boundaries drenched in strategy that kept Jesus focused on love and being love. If you find yourself feeling unsafe, ask yourself the following question: Are you in a safe community or a toxic community? A safe community takes an active pursuit, you have to seek it out, and you know when you find it because the people in the community follow Jesus and they are trustworthy in the following. They also encourage you to follow Jesus, and they walk in peace because they are filled with peace. It's also a safe space for you to express your feelings, and they allow you to have emotional moments, but they don't let you live there and pitch a tent in your feelings.

If that is all good and set in place, and you are still feeling unsafe, ask yourself: Are you walking in peace and filled with peace? Are you following Jesus intentionally and closely? Are you still dragging your bio behind you? What are you still holding on to that is keeping you far behind Jesus? Remember, peace isn't a feeling; it's a person. Are you spending time in the word, are you spending time in his presence, or are you still attached to your net? This will determine how closely you follow, and the closer you are, the better!

But if, after all this, you are still like, "Chari, I still feel unsafe and feel like I'm being attacked by the enemy and his nonsense!" then you should establish or re-establish your boundaries and make sure your strategy is in place. If you are looking for extra resources on boundaries, read everything ever written by Dr. Henry Cloud and Brené Brown. You can also spend some time studying the book of Proverbs, as it is pretty clear on how to navigate life and love and how to follow God well. For me, my days and my life are structured around how I can best love and be abundant in love in my following. And everything else I kindly say no to. I turn my phone off, I have a bedtime, my Sabbath is sacred, and my mornings start with the word. I guard my life with community and boundaries, so my life can be free to follow closely to peace; safe and secure and screened in peace, and that's the way I like it.

Nestled in a safe community.

Free of nets.

Following after peace closely.

Embracing security that is only found in Jesus.

Onward.

CHAPTER 5
HIS POV

How to deal with feeling insecure

Be you; everyone else is taken.

I've always loved writing and storytelling. Even as a young child, I was always fascinated with how stories were beautifully curated in newspapers and on film. Maybe the fascination is in my DNA, as I come from a long line of authors, storytellers, and educators. But I like to believe my desire to tell stories and curate moments is a God-dream that God, in his goodness, fashioned together so I could glorify him in my life. In fourth grade, I had access to a large printer in my elementary school because my mom taught at the school, so I got the idea to create my own magazine. The idea was to release one edition a week and give it away to students after school who were waiting for their buses and rides home. I did all the interviews and the writing, I did all the design and the layout, and I handled all the printing, stapling, and distribution. I was a one-kid team, and my hustle was legit! An English teacher in the school hooked me up with the extra paper from class, so every edition of my magazine was bright pink, purple, or blue. Each piece was fancy, occasionally glittered, and bedazzled. Rarely did I have to use regular printer paper, and every week people would ask for my magazine and ask to be part of what I was creating. I was living that hashtag-blessed life!

A few months into that school year, my dad got a great job opportunity that moved us to a new state and school, and the magazine was no more. But I was confident that I would somehow be able to continue my writing ventures in my new school. A few weeks into the new adventure, I was called in to speak to the reading and writing teacher; I was excited. This was my moment! I was going to pitch my magazine idea to her, but before I could, she began to tell me that I was failing both reading and writing and that the school was going to move me to the lower reading class. I thought maybe there had been some oversight; I was a good writer! I remember thinking, *I own my own magazine.* I knew my grammar was sketchy, but the writing was spot-on. Reading and writing were my favorite subjects. They had to have made a mistake! And so I asked her, with all the assurance and confidence in the world and a bit of a laugh, "Are you sure you have the right kid? I was already halfway through this textbook in my old school, and I had a good grade." She paused, leaned over, and began to assure me that she indeed had the right kid, and that very day she moved me into the class with the rest of the kids who had what she called a disability.

SPEAK LIFE

A bit of context: that season of my life was tough. My dad's new job was meant to give us a bump up in the financial situation, which was very much in the red. But, to make ends meet, we moved in with my grandparents to help us get ahead. In the new city, we lived in a not-so-great neighborhood, and we looked and dressed low budget. We moved from southern Michigan to southern Georgia, so the culture shock was extreme. Our school was racially charged, and as the city had an extreme racial divide in its schools and neighborhoods, almost every fight or schoolyard argument was saturated with a racial slur. This left the three Cuban kids far, far away from fitting in and, sadly, easy targets for ridicule. We also walked home every day because our family didn't have a car. As a result, we were bullied by the older kids and chased home every day. The magazine was all I had really had during that season prior to the move. It gave me confidence and purpose, and spoke to who I wanted to be, and now it was gone. I already felt inadequate and invisible as the "poor kid," the "not white kid" and the "not black kid," the "no-car kid," the "speaks another language" kid. And now I was the "dumb kid" and the "can't write or read kid."

Looking back now, I can see it was a stealthy attack of the enemy on my nine-year-old identity and confidence. It was an attack on the pillars that helped build my confidence and allowed me to feel secure and seen. Insecurity, the feeling of not being good enough, met me in this season, and it tried to speak its corrupted perspective over my heart and mind. But God saw me, and he saw fit to speak words directly into my feelings. He spoke life that outweighed the truth of my feelings with the truth of his word. And he did this through my grandmother and my mother, as they saw that I was struggling to see myself in a healthy way, so they went into full encouragement mode. Both my mom and grandmother were epic women of faith and accomplished educators who read with me daily and encouraged my writing. My mother specifically worked with kiddos who had reading disabilities and immediately used all her skills to get my confidence back to where it needed to be. They took me to the movies to spark my creativity and bought me magazines and journals to encourage my writing. They spoke words of life and scriptures over me, they had me memorize scripture, and then they taught me to speak those scriptures over myself:

I am a child of God. (1 John 3:2)

I am wonderfully made. (Psalm 139:14)

I am bold. (2 Corinthians 3:12)

I am blessed. (Ephesians 1:3)

I am light. (Matthew 5:14–16)

I am set apart. (1 Peter 2:9)

I am a conqueror. (Romans 8:37)

I am enough. (Colossians 2:10)

I am gifted. (1 Peter 4:10)

I am loved. (Romans 8:38–39)

Nowadays, people call these affirmations, but back in the day, this was just God's truth being spoken over my brokenness, his words eclipsing what others had spoken over me. His point of view, unpacked by the scriptures, shifted my perspective on how I saw God and how God saw me. And in that outpouring of love and scripture, the foundation of my identity was poured. My family did everything they could to make sure I saw myself through the filter of love and the scriptures and not my feelings or my circumstance. They spoke purpose over my lack and insecurities, and what the enemy meant to make me feel more insecure eventually backfired into building a strong identity. It shifted my perspective and the way I saw myself so drastically that the school had me meet with the school counselor because they could not figure out how I had bounced back so fast.

The world, just like my elementary school, will never

understand a Jesus-like bounce-back, as it's rooted in life being spoken over you, a firm identity, and seeing your life as a truly blessed life. A blessed life that seeks after God's *voice* when you feel overwhelmed.

A blessed life that seeks after God's *presence* when you feel lonely.

A blessed life that seeks after God's *word* when you feel fearful.

A blessed life that seeks after God's *ways* when you feel unsafe.

And a blessed life that seeks after God's *point of view* when you feel insecure.

This view of a blessed life ignites bounce-backs that preach the good news, heal the sick, and impact the world with no worldly credentials. And that's the kind of life that insecurity can't thrive in.

This world is filled to the brim with circumstances that can make anyone and everyone feel inadequate, but Jesus's life and solutions for lack of confidence are timeless. Jesus does not swipe left or right; he chooses you. Jesus doesn't send you a yearly performance review to tell you how you've missed the mark; he's already equipped you to be successful right where you are. Sadly, most see Jesus or their faith as a last resort when confidence is low, or when their emotions are out of control. Others see Jesus or their faith in Jesus as something they engage on major holidays. But understanding Jesus's point of view on who he is, on who you are in him, and on what you were meant for are the only ways you can truly live out godly confidence that karate-chops insecurity.

WALK IN A FIRM IDENTITY

Jesus had tons of reasons to lack confidence, as well as experiencing circumstances that could have and should have caused him to feel inadequate. Just to name a few: Jesus grew up in a not-so-nice town, and I'm certain that the whispers of his immaculate conception had been long replaced with the assumption that he was a product of an affair of sorts. Jesus also didn't give off blessed vibes. His birth story was sketchy, his town was sketchy, and his life and day job were not the type of things that would eventually set him up for the rabbi position he would step into. He wasn't known as the smartest or from the best family, but still, he had a hunger to read and learn, and his wisdom astounded people. Jesus was every bit the "poor kid," the "weird kid," and the "thinks his dad is God kid." I am certain that insecurity was every bit a feeling he had to navigate, as he had a hefty list of things that told him daily that he should be insecure and lack confidence in his life and in his goals. Yet he remained confident and secure.

We see Jesus's confidence reignited in the garden of Gethsemane when he ran to his heavenly Father to gain a heavenly reminder of his purpose and his identity. We saw his unshaken confidence when he was twelve, in the temple, and being dragged back to Nazareth toward his triggers and struggles. Jesus also kept his confidence intact in the wilderness as he faced the enemy, and when he later handpicked his community. And you can see it again when Jesus set up his boundaries from a place of peace, regardless of what his family wanted of him, or what the religious leaders of the time expected from him. Jesus's confidence remained strong when he felt overwhelmed, lonely, fearful, and attacked by the enemy, because his identity was firmly planted in who his father said he was, and that was the Son of the Living God. Jesus didn't lose his confidence or self-worth because his point of view was firmly set on how his heavenly Father saw things, and we should do the same! We should see life and the world, relationships and people, in the same way Jesus did.

Jesus's identity wasn't founded on where he was from or what his parents had produced. His confidence and his identity were secure and unshakable because they were shaped in seasons in which he was invisible and hidden, and that gave his heavenly Father space to safely speak life and scripture and purpose over him when life and feelings were speaking something very different. Recap: when Jesus was baptized, the heavens opened, and the voice of the living God, the creator of the universe, thundered and called Jesus his son and then said he was pleased with him. I am going to believe that because Jesus didn't pass out from the shock, this was not the first time he had experienced this level of love and affirmation. As a result, Jesus walked in confidence, and that assurance was a complete reflection of an open heaven over his life.

Jesus's identity was rooted in the truth that his heavenly Father was pleased with his ongoing obedience to embrace solitude, wildernesses, the garden, and ultimately the cross! This was life-changing and powerful. Look, I'm certain the life of Jesus wasn't easy, but it was transformational and thriving, not only for Jesus but for everyone who would encounter his life and for those who would one day hear his story. And I wonder, what would our lives look like if we walked in that kind of confidence and life-changing self-worth? Confidence in the world makes others feel less, but when you look at Jesus's confidence, you see it made others feel empowered to follow truth because he was empowered by God, the Father, the Holy Spirit, and the solitude and life found in both. If you look back on all the stories we've chatted about so far, Jesus wasn't in the business of telling people how awesome he was, but instead how he lived his life and served and loved others spoke to how awesome God was and is.

Walking in godly assurance and confidence feels like always having the best player on your team, no matter what sport you're playing. No matter how many times the game is changed or what the weather looks like, you step into every game knowing you're going to win. Also, walking in true confidence and navigating insecurity like Jesus doesn't mean you think you're super awesome; it means you know how awesome

God is, and that's your foundation. You don't feel unworthy when circumstances or people try to cut you down because the God that created the world knows you by name and calls you his! The same God also speaks life over you through your community and nudges you forward as you follow the path of peace. Confidence like Jesus's isn't built over time; it's imparted over conversation with the creator through scripture, prayer, solitude, and community.

How have you tried to build your self-worth? Success will tell you your worth and adequacy is based on what you do. A relationship will tell you your worth and adequacy is based on how you love. Social media will tell you your worth and adequacy are based on who follows you. But when you devote your life to Jesus, your worth and feelings of adequacy are found in what he has done, in how much he loves you, and in following his path. And what you will experience is a life full of blessings that feel like love, joy, peace, patience, and everything in between.

UNDERSTAND THE BLESSING

In Matthew 5, Jesus is now in his thirties and full of godly confidence curated and homegrown in the life spoken over him by his heavenly Father. Jesus steps into ministry with a firm identity and preaches one of his most famous sermons: the Sermon on the Mount. It's the first major stage of his ministry days, and it's where he first famously talks about being salt and light. It's where he tells everyone to love their neighbors and turn the other cheek. But he kicks things off with the beatitudes, eight proverb-like proclamations without narrative, and they hit a hard reset on what living a blessed life really means and looks like.

- Blessed are the poor in spirit, for theirs is the kingdom of heaven.
- Blessed are those who mourn, for they will be comforted.
- Blessed are the meek, for they will inherit the earth.
- Blessed are those who hunger and thirst for righteousness, for they will be filled.
- Blessed are the merciful, for they will be shown mercy.
- Blessed are the pure in heart, for they will see God.
- Blessed are the peacemakers, for they will be called children of God.
- Blessed are those who are persecuted because of righteousness, for theirs is the kingdom of Heaven.

Jesus, the unqualified rabbi with an unqualified crew, shouldn't be preaching with confidence. But the guy from a sketchy town and with a sketchy birth story is perched on a hill surrounded by people; he's high enough to be heard clearly and to see their problems, their worries, and their insecurities; and he's moved to compassion. He understands what it feels like to be insecure, and so he unleashes what life would look like if everyone walked their lives out under the shade of security and blessing the way he has. Not the kind of security, success, and blessings experienced by the ultra-successful or the rich. Not the kind of success and blessings experienced by the happily engaged or the family full of children. But the blessings and security only experienced with godly confidence found in speaking life over your heart and mind and a firm identity.

And so we find Jesus, the rabbi with no famous religious guy backing and every reason to feel insecure, teaching the masses. Yet he confidently stands on a hill and lays out how to live a blessed life, a confident life, and a secure life. And to those who have already experienced Jesus it is no surprise that his words turn everyone's world upside down. If you look closely, you'll see that Jesus, in the first eight sentences of his message, shows us how he dealt with insecurity. As in his thirty-plus years of life, the world has actively tried to tell him who he was, and in response, he told the world who his Father said he was and then unleashed his Father's ways and purposes and plans on the masses.

Jesus does this in eight sentences that blow up every preconceived notion about what it looks like to be blessed. He shows that blessings aren't connected to what you can do or what you can confidently make, or how successful or educated you are. True self-worth and security is found in God. He tells the world, "Hey, you're doing this whole success and blessings thing all wrong! And I can show you the right way." In those eight sentences Jesus did not say blessed and secure and confident are those with money and good jobs. He didn't say blessed and secure and confident are those who have a large following or worldly recognition. And he didn't say blessed and secure and confident are those who walk through life with no struggle. Nope!

He was saying that even though the world says that if you want to inherit a kingdom, you have to be born into the right family, and even though religion says that if you want to inherit the kingdom, you must be the holiest, the most righteous, true confidence, assurance, and security were found in the opposite. He then invited the unlikely, the broken, the unworthy, and the inadequate to confidently join his kingdom by saying:

- Blessed are those who drop their nets and follow.
- Blessed are those with feelings, for they will be comforted.
- Blessed are those who are walking in humility, for they will find success.
- Blessed are those who find their significance and provision in me; their hunger will be satisfied.
- Blessed are those who forgive and show empathy, for they will reap what they sow.
- Blessed are those who pursue wholeness, for they shall see God.
- Blessed are those who experience the Prince of Peace and, in response, sow peace.

- Blessed are those who struggle and face difficult circumstances because they have chosen to follow me; they will experience a heavenly perspective.

Of course, these are the Chari version of these verses, but Jesus was shaking the perspective of everyone who assumed their firm identity and confidence were attached to things, people, or circumstances. He was dropping bombs on insecurity and unleashing truth about godly confidence and true blessings on the masses.

Blessed are those who drop their nets and follow.

Do you want to walk in confidence? Do you want to experience the blessings of God that allow you to walk in confidence? Then you need a firm identity that isn't built on sand or shifting with the tides of culture. If you want to walk in a firm identity with Godly confidence, you first must drop whatever you *feel* makes up your identity to truly follow Jesus. In my world, that means I have had to lay down my dreams and my gifts, also known as the things I put in my bio and that identify me to the world: wife, pastor, creative director, author, and reluctant millennial. I lay down who I love and who loves me. All relationships, and journeys, I lay them down. It means every puzzle piece in my personality and my thought patterns; I lay them down to follow Jesus and pick up his ways of living and loving. This does not mean I lose myself in following Jesus; it means I find myself in following blessing.

TAKEAWAY: *A firm identity is a blessing and fights off insecurity.*

Blessed are those with feelings, for they will be comforted.

God created us with emotions and will totally use those feelings for his glory. But not having the right people speaking over your feelings can be detrimental to your growth and confidence. Jesus knew that insecurity was debilitating, and if not navigated with the right community speaking life over us, it could keep us stuck emotionally. So here we find Jesus reiterating the fact that your feelings are important and valid. Feelings are a gift from God, but healthy feelings are a gift that must be cultivated under the shade of life-giving words and time with Jesus and in our community. He was taking time here to encourage all the feelers out there and letting us know that he's going to send comfort by way of community and his presence.

TAKEAWAY: *Having others speak godly truth and life over your feelings is a blessing, and it fights off insecurity.*

Blessed are those who are walking in humility, for they will find success.

Success isn't winning; it's thriving. Jesus, in this beatitude, was giving us the cheat sheet for how to walk in godly confidence and to see it all as a blessing. Jesus was saying, "You don't have to strive for success; just abide and walk with me."

He'd been walking this principle out for like thirty years, and now he was showing the world. If you are struggling with imposter syndrome in your life, in your job, all while trying to reach the mountaintop of success, stop. Ask yourself, am I truly abiding in God's words and his truth about me and for me? Am I walking humbly, knowing it is God who keeps me secure and who truly sees me? If not, pause. God wants to see you thrive in life, not survive your life. And walking in humility—or what I like to call "throwing your hands up" and letting God take the wheel of your life—will plant your identity in Jesus. And this level of surrender keeps you from striving for temporal successes that don't have an eternal impact. It keeps you from worrying about things that in the long run won't matter! So walk humbly and learn to be okay with the feeling of letting go. Because if you fully let go of your perceptions of what will make you blessed and confident, there will be a shift in your heart and mind from striving to thriving. And thriving is the outcome you want.

TAKEAWAY: *Being able to understand and walk out humility is a blessing, and it fights off insecurity.*

Blessed are those who find their significance and provision in me; their hunger will be satisfied.

Jesus knew the crowd lived hungry, and not just physically, but emotionally and spiritually. They were hungry to be seen and valued, and hungry to be free of the trappings of the Roman occupation. Many of us hunger for the same kind of freedom, so we root our significance in what we assume will provide us that freedom, and we live discontentedly in the process. Jesus understood their hunger as he'd just had it attacked by the enemy. Jesus walked out of the wilderness, and not only was it overwhelming, scary, lonely, and super unsafe, but it had the possibility of shaking his identity. Yet he understood that his provision and perspective came from the Father, and so his confidence remained intact, and he was able to walk out not only in the power of the Holy Spirit but in humility. Jesus had a hunger and feelings just like us! A hunger to be seen and known, and that hunger was satisfied in the presence and in words of truth and life spoken to him and over him by his heavenly Father. If you want to combat insecurity, double-check what your significance is rooted in, where your perspective is focused, and what you're feeding your life with.

BIG TAKEAWAY: *Contentment is a blessing, and it fights off insecurity.*

Blessed are those who forgive and show empathy, for they will reap what they sow.

Jesus understood that insecurity grows in the soil of offense, and it's watered by unforgiveness. He'd dealt with tons of things said to him and about him. He was a target for insults! But when Jesus looked upon the masses of people, he knew that many were missing out on living a confident, blessed life due to unforgiveness. If you are feeling insecure when you walk into the room, if you are worried about what others are saying about you, it could be because you are offended by something someone said or did to you. You may even be mad at yourself.

This is where you are going to have to do some digging. Jesus lived a life where others had nothing nice to say about him, yet he chose empathy and kindness and love. He lived out the scriptures and purpose that had been set in place by his Father, not the words spoken over him by the world. Jesus expressed this truth when he faced the enemy in the wilderness and said, "Man shall not live on bread alone, but on every word that comes from the mouth of God." What bread are you ingesting? What words are you living out and sowing? Whatever it is, you will reap it back in one way or another; make sure you are sowing love!

BIG TAKEAWAY: *Walking in forgiveness is a blessing, and it fights off insecurity.*

Blessed are those who pursue wholeness, for they shall see God.

Wholeness is not a destination; it's a road we have to travel daily. Jesus looked out at those gathered to hear him speak, and they were sick, lame, poor, and not what the world would perceive as people on the road toward wholeness. But sitting at the feet of Jesus's words is exactly what wholeness looks like! It's a daily engagement of his truth found in the scriptures, his presence, and his ways that give us confidence and security to walk out wholeness like a boss. Insecurity, like fear, will blur your perception and show you that without Jesus you can arrive at total security and confidence, but that's a lie. It's something you must walk toward every day, all day. And it's on the trek toward wholeness, in pursuing Jesus, where confidence and a firm identity are built while you walk and talk with God. This trek, this road to wholeness, is what keeps you focused on love, being love, and producing love.

BIG TAKEAWAY: *Wholeness found in the pursuit of Jesus is a blessing and fights off insecurity.*

Blessed are those who experience the Prince of Peace and, in response, sow peace.

Confidence, the type of Tom Brady confidence that wins the Super Bowl of life over and over again, even into our old age and well past our prime, is only found in Jesus, the Prince of Peace. And so if you want to combat insecurity, attach yourself to peace, the person. You do this by saying yes to filtering your words, actions, beliefs, and feelings the way Jesus did. There is no peace as a feeling apart from the peace that is the person, and that person is Jesus Christ. If you want to feel secure and confident, the ways of Jesus will lead you. The ways of Jesus will show you how to walk into chaotic circumstances and respond with patience and compassion. Jesus looked out on the crowds and didn't see their brokenness as a deterrent but as an opportunity to be love and show love. Peace lives like that. Peace is a person with very real responses that keep your words and responses focused off your struggles with unhealthy emotions and instead on Jesus and healthy emotions cultivated in the Holy Spirit. You can't make peace; you can only abide it. **BIG TAKEAWAY:** *Abiding in peace is a blessing, and it fights off insecurity.*

Blessed are those who struggle and face difficult circumstances because they have chosen to follow me; they will experience a heavenly perspective.

Jesus sat on a hill, surrounded by a massive crowd who were living in a violently occupied territory and facing real-world sicknesses and deficits. They had every reason to feel insecure about life, and provision, and their personal self-worth. Yet Jesus flipped the script yet again to say, hey, your everyday struggles found in life and in walking out your faith don't mean you're not blessed; they mean you're alive! Having a life with no storms or struggles doesn't equate to having a blessed life. Having a life that doesn't ever encounter difficult circumstances doesn't fight off insecurity and build your identity. Insecurity and struggles remind us that we are human and in need of a savior; they remind us that we need to drop our nets and that God is always close and ready to comfort us.

God uses struggle to remind us to walk in humility and find our identity and wholeness in the presence and words and forgiveness of the Prince of Peace. Struggle isn't always bad. Struggle is a character builder that God can use for his glory to sharpen us and mature us into who he has called us to be. It can also be used as a space where we learn to hear God's voice clearly and the perfect stomping ground to fail forward. Jesus struggled, the people surrounding him on that hill struggled, and God was still glorified.

BIG TAKEAWAY: *Struggle can be a blessing, as it fights off insecurity.*

I know some of these beatitudes feel backward, but Jesus's life wasn't lived out to make us comfortable; it was lived out and sacrificed to make us whole. Whole and focused on building a firm identity in God the Father and finding comfort in the right places. Whole and walking humbly, with an understanding of where to find provision and significance. Whole within a community that exudes love and peace; and whole because they are following closely to peace, even when it's hard, even in the struggle.

If you find yourself in the struggle, if you find yourself feeling insecure about life, know this: the Bible describes the Holy Spirit as a still, small voice, a whisper. And that whisper is trying daily to speak life over you. Sometimes life and truth will come from the scriptures or your community, and other times, it will be a grandmother or your mom doing the talking. My question to you is, can you hear it? Can you hear the truth being spoken over your life? If not, what is so loud that you can't hear it? What is close enough to drown out that still, small voice? In moments when I feel insecure, I run to those I trust the most to help me hear the Lord clearly.

When the static of insecurity is clogging my ability to hear from the Holy Spirit, I'll remove all the draining apps on my phone and take a break from social media. I'll fast from television and movies. I'll stop listening to music that doesn't speak the truth of God's word in those moments, and I'll focus on whatever I need to do in my day to quiet the noise of insecurity that tries to tell me that whatever God has gifted me with is not enough. If you are having trouble hearing the Holy Spirit, you must turn everything else off. You can't maintain a firm identity if you keep detaching yourself from the person who gives you your confidence.

Most of us spend our lives never realizing we are one of a kind. Most of us will never realize that the God of creation sent his Son to this earth to beat death to an unrecognizable state so that we could be confident in who we are and confident that we are loved beyond words. We will try to fight off insecurity by chasing temporal successes that the world calls blessed or confident. We will do this unknowingly with people and moments that make us feel loved, seen, and secure. And we will do this because the words we've allowed to shape us are broken and produced through a filter of brokenness.

Jesus walked in confidence and slayed insecurity because his life was not defined by what others spoke about him but by what his Father declared over him. And God the Father calls you his; you are his child, so be confident in this. If you want to combat the feeling of insecurity, the lie that we are unseen and not enough, choose to speak the words of God over your heart and mind. Graft your identity to Jesus's life in such a way that people are drawn to your life—drawn to your life because you're abiding in God's ways, which are rooted in scripture and fertilized by love.

Speak life.

Root your identity in Jesus.

Stand strong.

Read the beatitudes often.

Be anxious of nothing.

Onward.

CHAPTER 6

HIS PACE

How to deal with feeling anxious

The pace of Jesus is the most underrated thing about him.

I live in a permanent state of anxiety or uneasiness that some-times causes me to feel restless and tense. It causes my heart to beat in a weird way, and when my anxiety is really bad it triggers my asthma. This doesn't make me less of a Christian or mean I don't work out my emotions with Jesus as my model; it just means I'm human. Yes, I'm well aware that I'm writing a book about having healthy feelings and finding a solution to those feelings through Jesus and his awesomeness. But you need to know the truth about my struggle; I'm not giving you a solution I heard somewhere, but solutions that breathe life into my emotions when I feel like they are too much to bear.

Besides Jesus and his awesomeness, I, of course, have developed practical strategies to help with my anxiety, like making sure I'm rested before travel and that I take time to decompress before having to spend time with more people. And if I have spent an entire day pouring out in some way, I make sure to be alone somewhere and go to bed early so I can fully recharge. I intentionally find spaces where I can quiet my mind without interruptions to settle my heart and mind back to Jesus, my center. I also embrace the spiritual gift of organization in my life and my schedule to make sure things don't feel chaotic or trigger my anxiety.

I also need at least two cups of coffee before nine a.m. or I tend to unravel. One time I fasted from coffee, and my boss told me to go make myself a cup or she would fire me. I took that as the Lord telling me my coffee needs were okay, and I've just embraced it. When I'm feeling really anxious, I get up from my desk, walk outside, and jump into my pool fully clothed—a perk of working remotely and living in Florida. Jumping in the pool in my entire work outfit makes me laugh and allows me to stop taking myself too seriously. I also have a counselor I call, pastor friends I rely on, a thriving community, an incredible husband, and family and friends who all know me, know this about me, and help me work through it. But sometimes, some situations catch me up. The cave in Northern California was one of those situations.

Due to my anxiety, and the fact that I'm accident prone, I don't really do hiking excursions, outside adventures, or traveling to anything that Gen Z might deem an appropriate location for a spontaneous TikTok dance. But for some reason, in the heart of the COVID pandemic and on the mend from the COVID virus, I decided the best thing I could do, with my breathing treatments in tow, was take a family vacation to Northern California with my husband, my sister's entire family, and my cousins. And when I say "take a trip," I mean we were going to do the whole drive up the Pacific Coast Highway, venture into Muir Woods, take pictures by the Golden Gate, visit Alcatraz, have a nice dinner in Napa Valley—the whole shebang! My iPhone was doing that whole listening to all of my conversations thing and, in response, began to send me ideas for all of the excursions in Northern California that I'd mentioned.

My niece Saylah is super adventurous and an athlete and very much a capturer of moments. So when a very well-known cave excursion popped up on my Instagram feed, I suggested we go as a family so Saylah could get cool pictures. Everyone was excited, and we bought tickets for what the guide eventually referred to as the Devil's Cavern. As someone who hates closed-in spaces and weird smells, this wasn't my go-to type of adventure. But I love my niece; she's one of my greatest gifts in life! God didn't give me a daughter, but he gave me Saylah. My sister laughs that she somehow had a child who looks and acts just like me, so I wasn't going to miss an opportunity to make a lasting memory with my mini-me. So I took one for the team, overlooked the countless red flags embedded within this excursion, and tried to get mentally ready.

The next morning everyone got dressed and ready to go to the caves. I, as usual, was dressed in my all-black Johnny Cash attire, but as if Johnny Cash were spending winter in New York City and not winter in Northern California. Also, because COVID had done a number on my lungs, and I was still on substantial breathing treatments, I carried my emergency inhaler everywhere. Everywhere except the cave expedition, because I left it in my other jacket. I just didn't know this until I found myself needing it deep inside the Devil's Cavern…but I don't want to get ahead of myself.

It was a significant drive into the mountains to find this cave situation. It was also a significant trek to get our tickets. And those walkie walks were then sprinkled with a legitimate hike down a mountain to the lake, which led to a ride in a boat across a lake. And then a drive up the mountain into the cave via a school bus that looked more like a murder bus from the seventies. Everyone was laughing and taking pictures in the peaceful mountain air. I, on the other hand, immediately regretted the decision to come here, and I could feel the anxiety brewing. My anxiety is a butthole and tends to steal my peace and cause my patience to evaporate. And in these moments, it begins to trigger my asthma. Usually when this happens, I always default to the same thing—I start taking very aggressive deep breaths and working through my anxiety with prayer and breathing and my inhaler, and an attitude of gratitude. But in this moment, there was a sploosh of panic. Which is also kind of my MO.

The walk down to the lake was longer than normal because the waterline was lower than usual. I noticed that as everyone in our crew was laughing walking down to the lake, the people walking back up the hill, the same ones who had just visited the cave, looked miserable and worn out. Everyone walking with me toward the lake was happy and laughing and taking pictures. Everyone walking back up the mountain looked tired, hot, and worked over! It was winter; why were these people hot and removing their jackets? Everyone kind of laughed it off, except me! Any excitement I had about the hike was fading to zero.

We got to the boat and, shockingly, the ride was magical. My anxiety dissipated, my peace returned, my breathing regulated, and my patience level went all the way back up to ten. The air was crisp, and the sky was the most beautiful blue I'd ever seen in my entire life. It was as if the blue was ricocheting off the green forest and red clay. It looked like a painting! I couldn't believe I'd found this excursion; everyone was happy and thanked me, and Saylah looked so joyful. At that moment, whatever anxiety was trying to creep in was replaced with joy and gratitude and a core memory that would last a lifetime.

Then we landed on the shore that led to the cave, and the seventies murder bus awaited us, and the driver looked like there might or might not have been a very low-budget whiskey in his coffee cup.

In case you missed it in my roller coaster story in chapter one, I have super claustrophobic vibes. I haven't been diagnosed with this phobia; I just like to slow-dance with irrational fears, and I assume I'm claustrophobic because it said so on WebMD. Also, I don't like elevators, crowded spaces, weird smells, or places that could trigger my asthma. Why did I think going into a dark cave would be a good idea? I'm so glad you asked. Because I wanted to give my niece a memory that she'd one day remember when I was long gone. And did I do that? Unfortunately, yes!

When the metal door of death swung open, you could see a dark hallway that eventually opened into a cavern. I pretended I didn't want to quit this dumb idea immediately; Saylah was there and excited, and the whole family seemed ready to go! Once we got into the first cavern, I was fine; in the second cavern, not so much. It was then in what they called the Devil's Cavern, surrounded by what the brochure called a "mysterious and unique world of exquisite rock formations," that all hell broke loose.

Me: *(in a panicked tone to the guide)* Where are the windows?

Guide: *(stunned yet chuckling)* Ma'am, there are no
windows.

Me: Well then, how do we get out?

Guys, guys! Why was I asking about windows in a cave?
Also, was I going to jump out of a window? The entire group
tour just stared at me, as, of course, we are under the ground,
and there are no windows, and the only way out was through
the Devil's Cavern.

Guide: Ma'am, are you okay?

Me: *(absolutely not okay)* I'm fine, I'm fine, we're all
fine! Guys, are we fine?

This is where I could no longer control my anxiety, and I
reached for my inhaler. And well, it was nowhere to be found,
just like my peace and patience! My inhaler was at home; my
peace and patience—well, I'd surrendered them to the cave.
So, of course, I did the rational thing anyone who is overcome with anxiety would do: I started to strip off my jacket
and sweater in the cave because I couldn't breathe. I turned
into Will Ferrell from *Talladega Nights* and started stripping
and saying crazy things! My sister, who is also a bit dramatic
and also fake claustrophobic, started to panic a bit, so she
grabbed my hand lovingly, the way only a sister could, and
then she said in a panicked tone, attempting to be calm:

My Sister: Chari, look at me. It's okay; I'm here with
    you.
(enter husband into the story)
Husband: Yeaaaah, that's really not going to help her!
    Trust me!
Me: Why are you holding my hand? We got to get
    out of here; I can't breathe!

The next fifteen minutes were a total blur as my sister and I ran through all the photo ops and the rest of the caverns trying to get out, followed by our family and the guide. Once the door swung open to the outside air where I would find refuge, I found a tiny, sketchy stairwell down the mountain. I then realized why everyone leaving this cave looked like they wanted to die. Not only had I talked my family into a cave, but now we had to hike back down this mountain via the smallest stairs ever, and they had no rail or safety fence. Then we had to get back into that sketchy bus to the magical boat that no longer felt magical as my asthma was in full swing. We then hiked back up the mountain and drove the long ride home. This is still hands down one of the worst anxiety attacks I've ever had, and sadly it happened in the most magical place ever, with the people I love the most, all while trying to build memories.

I'm not sure what your anxiety is triggered by, but mine is usually triggered by crowds of people and circumstances out of my control. And that trigger causes me to fly through life and miss out on rest for my soul and people I love. Full disclosure, not only am I WebMD-certified claustrophobic and a tad bit of a control freak, but I am an extreme introvert with an awkward dose of social anxiety that rears its ugly head on occasion. And it causes me to say no to things I love, people I care about, and potential memories that I would love to make. My pace is unhealthy, and at times rooted in my anxiety. I'm a real fun time, guys! All that to say, I didn't have to dig too deep into the scriptures to see how Jesus navigated crowds of people and extreme circumstances, as most stories found in the Gospels are his how-to guides on walking at his pace. A pace that doesn't bypass hurting people or get burned out, and this is the pace we must also walk if we want to navigate our emotions in a healthy way.

JESUS'S PACE RESTS

We see Jesus model this pace while still fully seeing people and throat-punching all levels of anxiety in Matthew 8. Jesus's disciples, at this point in the story, have seen him teach multitudes and heal a paralyzed person. They have witnessed Jesus heal a man with leprosy, and then they saw him heal Simon Peter's mother-in-law's fever. There had been no request too big or too small for Jesus, and the supernatural stuff hasn't just been random; it's been personal and up close and impacting! So, when Jesus tells his disciples in Matthew 8 to get in the boat with him and go to the next shore, in a sea that is known as a storm magnet, they didn't even think twice.

During their crossing, it says in the Mark 4 telling of this story that a "furious squall came up," and the waves were so intense they were breaking over the boat. Again, these are fishermen, people who have done waves and storms before, yet at this moment, they totally freak out. Like we all do sometimes—or like I do in caves—they forgot Jesus was with them, and they forgot Jesus is the best at getting us through temporal circumstances with supernatural solutions. The Bible says that the boat was covered in waves, and Jesus in the middle of the storm was fast asleep on a pillow at the back of the boat. And here is where we find the first big driver of his pace.

If you want to move at the pace of peace, the way Jesus did, you have to embrace rest.

Jesus didn't just rest when he had a chance just because they were walking all over the countryside; rest was a way of life for him. His Sabbaths were sacred, and his life was propelled by rest. For Jesus and us as believers, the Sabbath isn't a day off or the day you stay home to do laundry. The Sabbath is sacred and holy and transcends time and space and allows our heart and mind to focus back on the creator after a week of toiling. Also, rest is not a thing that was only in place for the Jewish people and is no longer needed in our lives; it's a Jesus thing, a Christian thing that has been eliminated in today's culture. And if we want to fight anxiety and win, we need to position rest at the forefront of our lives.

For me this looks like sunset on Friday nights, when I make dinner for my family, we light a few candles, and then we take a moment to pray and take communion in our home together. We thank God for the week and give him back the day, and reset our focus on his pace in the midst of the busy world we live in. Sometimes we invite friends over; sometimes, it's just our little family, but our Sabbath is God's, and we fight as a family to keep it that way.

We also don't fill it with activities—and not in a religious way, but in an intentional way. We purposefully have fun, sleep in, leave our phones in the other room, and take a day to just be thankful for all God has done during the week. We have purposeful conversations and talk about what God is doing in our lives and what our dreams are for the next season. If you don't make rest a rhythm in your life, it will sit on the shelf of your life as a reward, and the rest that is rewarded will never feel like true rest; it will feel like rehab.

I noticed this a few years ago when my husband, who loves being on boats and in tropical places, talked me into going on a cruise to rest. Day two of the cruise was like the Hunger Games—watching people sign up for excursions to help them rest. But none of those excursions sounded like rest to me; they sounded like more doing, more work. So as the masses of people fought over Jet Skis and zip lines, jungle hikes, and animal encounters, I found a quiet beach that everyone had abandoned to fake rest, and we enjoyed the stillness that I needed to quiet the anxious storms and waves that frequent my mind.

Unlike me, Jesus didn't need a beach to quiet his mind and rest because he was always able to quiet himself and rest. His pace was rooted in peace and patience and the ways of heaven because he engaged that level of sacred rest every week. And yet we find the disciples in the storm freaking out!

Epic recap: the waves were huge and crashing over the boat, the disciples were scared and screaming, and Jesus was still at peace and unbothered. "Help! Save us! Teacher, don't you care if we drown?!" is what they woke Jesus up with, and so Jesus, now awake, bypasses the people freaking out and the boat he's on and rebukes the wind: "Quiet! Be still!" Jesus, in the middle of a storm that came out of nowhere, was asleep on a pillow, unbothered and at peace. If this is not a cheat sheet for how to deal with anxiety-inducing situations, I don't know what is. If you are feeling anxious, surrounded by a storm in your life, and surrounded by your friends freaking out, don't assess the emotional people! Take a moment and rest in the fact that Jesus is with you! And if you need to go to the back of the boat, grab a pillow!

When the storms of life hit, it's okay to take a moment and recenter yourself. It's okay to look at the person you're in a tough situation with at work and say, "Hey, I need a moment to process. Can we circle back on this tomorrow?" I understand that stressful things happen all the time, but they don't necessarily need to happen to you. Everything isn't storms and waves; most things are just life lived in a broken world. When the storms and waves come, remember you are in the boat with Jesus, and Jesus is in full rest mode, and you should be too. When you are walking at the pace of peace, the pace of Jesus that is rooted in a sacred place of rest, you can react like Jesus to anxious moments, and not like the disciples.

I fully understand how backward this sounds, but Jesus was never in the business of making us comfortable; he has and always will be in the business of making us more Christ-like, as comfort breeds complacency. So rest. Cease trying to make everything work, and take a deep breath. Walk away from the problem or the person that is making you anxious and choose to handle the issue later. Choose rest. In his book *The Sabbath*, Rabbi Abraham Heschel said, "Labor is a craft, but perfect rest is an art. It is a result of an accord of body, mind, and imagination." And anxious without rest unravels that accord.

On a granular level this may mean you just need to take a nap, as I've just qualified naps being of the Lord! When I'm feeling anxious, sometimes it's triggered by lack of rest, and I legit just need a nap. Rest for you may look like a hard reset in your pace and a pause in your day or circumstance to remind yourself that Jesus is in the boat. Rest for someone else may look like taking a walk, a short vacation, a Netflix binge, a video game with a friend, or a date night. This doesn't mean you forget the storm; you're just reminding your *body, mind, and imagination* that you are not moved by storms. You are reminding your heart and mind that Jesus is in the boat, and Jesus is bigger, better, and badder than the storm. You are reminding your heart and mind that you are moved by the pace of peace, the pace of rest and patience, the pace of Jesus. And that pace not only navigates anxiety with healthy emotions, but it loves people and sees people along the way as well.

JESUS'S PACE SEES PEOPLE

Jesus has now been baptized, tempted, found in community, and preached his first big sermon. And what meets him on the other side of these wins and the Matthew 8 storm are tons of hurting people. He had emotional and desperate people who followed him everywhere he went. There was no reprieve from the peopling. They followed him across the sea and onto shores, into homes and into the temple. And one time the house he was teaching in was so packed they dropped a guy through the ceiling! Jesus also had to navigate vast numbers of sick people who were paralyzed, blind, lame, and covered with crazy infirmities like leprosy. And Jesus approached these people, spoke to them, healed them, and was kind to them. And most of these people had been shunned by society and their families, and Jesus was the first person in a long time actually to see them as people and not as problems.

When you're overcome with feelings and anxiety is leading the charge, people will always be a problem—especially people who are draining, desperate, and in need of a savior. After Jesus quieted the storm and the disciples changed their underwear, they were met on the shoreline by a very scary dude! This man was demon-possessed, naked, scratching his eyes out, and running around a cemetery naked with a legion of demons. It was so intense of a situation that after Jesus freed this man from his possession, the town he lived in told Jesus, "Yeah, we are going to need you and your homies to leave!" Here's the tea: Jesus's method of healing the demoniac scared those living in the town. Jesus freed this man, and it was amazing, but he also sent the legion of demons into a group of pigs, which then jumped off a cliff! Jesus's method of healing messed up how they made money, and what they perceived as their livelihood. Busy people, and busy people focused on money, won't see the miracle, as money is their God. Another way of putting it is people focused on their personal pace will miss Jesus's pace, and the ability to inspire freedom in others will be missed. Don't be those people.

Also, overly religious people will miss the miracles as well—like the Pharisees and Sadducees in Jesus's day who also followed him around to judge him and ask questions to discredit his miracles, his disciples, and his legitimacy as the Messiah. These are all things that would cause anyone with a pulse a good level of anxiety. But Jesus responded to each of these circumstances and people with eye contact and his undivided attention. He met these circumstances with a healthy dose of Holy Spirit emotions, like the compassion that healed people the religious felt were unworthy. He engaged gentleness that healed the sick people no one wanted to touch or be near. He exuded kindness that healed the demon-possessed that society left to run wild among the tombs, and of course, he was filled with extreme self-control as he did not get frustrated with everyone always pulling on him.

And even though Jesus had every reason to feel anxious as everyone and their mama was pulling on his time and emotional energy, he didn't seem affected or moved by their waves of emotion. When I read about the life of Jesus, I always see that he walked in peace and responded with patience. He was never in a hurry and never allowed people to rush him or let their temporal agenda outweigh the plans and purposes he was living out on behalf of his heavenly Father. He was always abiding in his Father's plans, which then resulted in a pace that kept his Sabbaths sacred and his truly seeing people and loving people non-negotiable. His pace, the walking in stride with his Father and the Holy Spirit, never allowed him to feel overwhelmed, lonely, fearful, unsafe, or insecure. And that is how I would like to live my life as well: a life that walks at the pace of peace, responding with patience and unmoved by people or circumstances.

People matter to God, and if you can't learn how to see people and love people like Jesus, you'll never be able to overcome anxiety like Jesus. You'll just blame people for all the reasons you are anxious. We are on this earth to be ambassadors of his love through our lives and our words and our emotions. Which, as a person riddled with social anxieties and irrational fears, I struggle with. But when we are walking at Jesus's pace:

his voice is loud,

his presence is tangible,

his words are clear,

his ways are accessible,

and his point of view is guiding you,

seeing people and loving people the way Jesus did becomes a priority and easy.

It's only difficult to truly love and see people, it's only difficult to find rest, when our voice is the loudest, and his presence is nowhere near us. It's only difficult when our temporal hungers that corrupt our significance and perspective cause us to forget his words, his ways, and his point of view. And that's when unhealthy emotions fill the gaps, and anxiety is a gap filler.

When the peopling becomes too much, when the storms just show up out of nowhere, when anxiety rears its ugly little head and tries to pressure you into a corner, choose the pace of Jesus. The pace that isn't rushed or hurried. The pace that doesn't rush by broken people but instead sees them as opportunity for freedom to reign and God to be glorified. The pace that rests in storms because of its rest in life. Anxiety cannot keep the pace of Jesus, as Jesus's pace rooted in rest, and peace and patience doesn't allow it to enter its race.

EMBRACE HIS PACE

Life is full of storms, whether you're on the water or the shore; like the disciples, you should not be startled or freaked out when people and circumstances show up out of nowhere. We live in a storm magnet full of imperfect people. Our responses to storms are often marred by shock and awe, yet they should be doused with peace and patience and rooted in rest, the type of peace and patience that is okay with you getting in the boat. The boat leads you to the purposes and plans that God has set in place for you. The boat leads you to more broken people in need of your love and the Jesus that you follow.

In moments when I see the clouds overhead and Jesus inviting me to a new shore, my normal default setting pace is "Where are the windows?" But when I'm functioning in the power of the Holy Spirit, in a healthy headspace, rested, and walking in peace and responding in patience, I grab my favorite pillow and head to the back of the boat. I won't lie; I don't always navigate this well—as I already admitted I live with social anxiety that I work through daily—but I do usually get in the boat. I just sometimes forget my pillow and forget Jesus is in the boat with me. But, thankfully, Jesus, in all his goodness, is not moved by anxiousness and always invites me back to watch him work his miracles and live out love, which then builds my faith and resets my emotions to a healthy setting of rest.

My favorite part of this story is Jesus's first act after the disciples woke him up. The very first thing he did was to tell the wind to shut its mouth! He was not overwhelmed or fearful; he did not feel unsafe or anxious. He was walking in the full authority of his heavenly Father and in the power of the Holy Spirit. I want to be so rested and walking at the pace of Jesus that when storms and circumstances and my emotions start freaking out, I can shut them up. He said, "Quiet! Be still!" The same wind and waves that came out of nowhere and shook and overwhelmed the boat were now quieted. The wind and the waves that caused panic and anxiety to the disciples were calmed at the sound of Jesus's voice. Have you ever been told to relax or calm down? It's demoralizing. Jesus was so gangster that he told the wind and waves to calm down and be still, and they did. That's the guy in the storm with us, the guy modeling a holy pace, and the guy who asked us to get in the boat with him.

Out of all the emotions I struggle with, anxiety is the one that bullies me the most, and is the toughest to overcome. Maybe it's because I loathe real and metaphorical boats, storms, and oceans filled with sharks, and I'm prone to panic when the waves show up. I think this is common—at least that's what the lady at my church who is a therapist says when I ask her questions on the low-low. When the anxiety kicks in, many times I have to get extra help to contend with my feelings and help me unravel what is not allowing me to truly rest and love people.

This looks like casually siphoning wisdom from my

therapist friends, reading a book about anxiety, or making an actual therapy appointment. Yep, if I've gotten in the boat and activated rest through weekly Sabbath and boundaries around my time and work, and I'm not speeding past people in the process, I'm great. But if somehow in the process, the waves get to be too much, I need to start waking people up, which is totally okay! When the disciples woke up Jesus, in Mark 4:35–41, he calmed the storm and then asked them, "Why are you so afraid? Do you still have no faith?" The goal is not to feel anxious, alone, in a boat, holding a pillow, hoping for the best. The goal is to remind yourself that Jesus is with you, and if need be, you can wake him up! Go to him; he is in the boat for a reason, and he is always willing and waiting to calm our storms. But just be ready for the questions that always come after the wake-up call.

Also, Jesus's response after the wake-up call is important, so don't miss it. He said, "Why are you so afraid?" which always reminds me that anxiety is rooted in fear, the liar, and the faith disruptor! In moments when rest isn't activating my peace the way it should, and people become my problem, I remember this moment and run back to Jesus. I will actually say out loud, "OKAY, JESUS, I need you to wake up. I need you to help me quiet this storm!" And it's in that crying out that I then begin to ask myself hard questions about what I am afraid of. Is my anxiety rooted in an attack on my significance, an attack on my perspective, or maybe even my hunger? And if I can't answer this question on my own, I get help. I ask my counselor, my pastor friends, my sunshine of a husband, and my inner circle.

Jesus in the storm showed me that he is always the solution for anxiety and that he has a supernatural, miracle-laced solution to help me walk with peace and respond with patience. And if I walk my life out with rest and love at the forefront of my heart and mind, I won't be such a gigantic target for anxiety's attack. See, the cave excursion showed me that my perspective is easy to attack. Especially if my perspective is focused on crowds and circumstances out of my control, it always causes bouts of fear in my heart and mind. It shifts my pace from peace and patience to anxiety and panic. That is my personal kryptonite that triggers my anxiety. What is yours? Write it down so that next time the waves crash over your boat you recognize it! Whatever your trigger is, the fix is still the same.

Engage rest like Jesus,
choose to see people like Jesus,
and then get in the boat.
Don't be anxious.
If needed, wake someone up.
Guard your heart.
Onward.

CHAPTER 7
HIS MOTIVES

How to deal with feeling offended

**You can't control offense,
but offended—that's all you.**

When I was nineteen, I was gifted with the position of the main worship leader of my church. This was huge for me, since at thirteen, I started serving in that ministry as the song lyrics/transparency girl. Back in the day, we did not have LED screens with words, but an overhead projector that pushed the words to a wall from a transparent plastic sheet that we'd write the song lyrics on. But at nineteen, they saw fit to upgrade me. I'd been faithful and moved from transparency to choir, from choir to soprano. Then they let me start playing my guitar and leading songs, and now, I was the worship leader! I was so proud of being entrusted with worship for our church, and I started building the team and bringing in edgy songs that had electric guitars! That first year the team grew significantly, and a true, healthy community was built within the team. This was life-altering in that season, as it was my first real experience with leadership and serving people and growing people in their gifting.

One Saturday, the pastor called a meeting with our entire team and invited us over to a house we'd never been to in a super nice neighborhood. It was fancy. We thought maybe it was an appreciation party, and we were all very excited. As the door opened, you could see a grand piano and crystal features throughout the foyer, and then the pastor asked that we all sit down as he wanted to introduce us to someone special.

We all gathered around the piano, and it was one of those moments that felt like it was in slow motion. I just looked around and saw my team and felt like this was what I was created for: to love people, grow people, and worship God. I was consumed with joy and gratitude, and it was a moment that will live rent-free in my mind forever. The pastor smiled at us all and stood in the middle of the room so we could all hear him. And then, without pause or pretense, he said, "I'd like to introduce you to Stephanie; she and her husband own this beautiful home. And as of tomorrow, she is our new worship leader."

There was no audible screeching halt, but there could have been. You could immediately hear the whispers and voices begin to ask questions.

"I'm sorry, what?"

"Could you repeat that?"

"What did he just say?"

"Which one is Stephanie?"

"Is this a joke?"

"Tomorrow?!"

"Chari, did you know this?"

I shook my head no in disbelief. The pastor then repeated the announcement with the same gusto and lack of self-awareness that he had utilized the first go-round. I just sat there in total shock. Stephanie (which isn't her real name, by the way) looked like JCPenney and 1982 had had a baby, and she was really excited about her new role. So much so that she immediately jumped in to tell us all about the changes she was going to make. My friend immediately stopped her mid-sentence, looked at the pastor, and said, "But what about Chari?" The pastor looked at me like I was an old shoe and said, "She'll be fine, she did a good job, but Stephanie is your new leader." Fade into Stephanie jumping back into her dissertation about worship, the changes she was going to make, and the inclusion of her grand piano in our sets. I don't remember what else was said because everything went blurry, and I just froze.

The next hour was spent with me sitting there in Stephanie's home, surrounded by my friends, with tears streaming heavily down my face. It was uncomfortable for everyone, especially Stephanie. She periodically would include me in her song ideas and ask my opinion, but I just stared into oblivion. Finally, I raised my hand and said, "Can I go now?" and before they could answer, I stood up to leave. The pastor patted me on the shoulder as I walked to the door, and he said to the group of people still in relative shock, "Don't worry, you'll see her tomorrow." First, he blindsided me with this shift and then he insulted me with his assumption. I was done. And I was thoroughly offended. He had thrown out a transgression that felt like too much to bear, and in response, I picked it up, put it in my pocket, named it, and took it home to knit it a sweater.

Stephanie lasted maybe six weeks. But my being offended lasted much longer. The offense produced anger and bitterness and unforgiveness in my heart. I showed up every week to help the worship experience, not with the zeal for God's house, but to be a middle finger to poor Stephanie week in and week out. I can't imagine how crazy it must have been to have been thrown into the lion's den with us, with no direction, no backing from a team, and the old guard still there staring you down from the other side of the stage. I never considered Stephanie's feelings or the team's feelings; I just focused on the injustice of it all. I never considered the pastor's decision or his motivation because, as usual, I always assumed the worst-case scenario. But I'd find out many years later that my inability to unpack motives and see circumstances as growth opportunities would be how offense strong-armed me toward living angry and bitter.

The truth is I was so focused on being hurt that I didn't realize I needed to be shaken a bit. I know now that my passion was being led by me and not by God. And that passion, unchecked, kept me offended. I was holding on to the gift and the position with a closed fist instead of holding on to Jesus. I am a bit embarrassed to admit this, but I was totally zealous for the gift instead of in love with the gift-giver, and that made me dangerous, especially in a worship position, where my worship needed to be directed to God and not the position. How it went down was horrible, offensive, insulting, and just wrong on every level. It was hands down one of the worst leadership decisions and executions of a decision I've ever witnessed or been a part of. But it wasn't the only time that I'd faced that kind of offense in life and in ministry.

Full disclosure, I didn't really learn my lesson, and I didn't surrender my zeal or choose forgiveness for a really long time. And God had to repeat a few of these lessons just to make sure I didn't miss them. But regardless of what God was trying to teach me, I lived offended and bitter and angry, and I saw people as the problem instead of an opportunity for me to choose love and experience personal growth. I never saw these moments of offense as a potential pruning of a relationship or position.

But now, with a clear view, I can say without a shadow of a doubt that God was working out how I see offense, how I am also an offender, and how God uses offense on the earth and in the kingdom. Even though I saw each offense as an insult to who I was trying to become or an attack on something I was holding way too tightly, offense on numerous occasions had polluted my passion and motives with unhealthy anger and total bitterness. And sadly, because I didn't learn the lesson at nineteen, I experienced the same kind of relational and professional offenses yet again at twenty-one, at twenty-eight, and thirty-three, thirty-six, and then again at forty, the type of offenses that God was using to teach me to truly see people, and truly see myself through his eyes.

Reality check: offense is going to happen whether you like it or not, but you don't have to live angry or bitter because of it. You don't have to take offense and make it part of who you are or why you act or respond a specific way. You have the power to not allow it to graft itself into your heart and mind and emotions. The biggest lie about offense is that the offense or the offender holds power! But you hold power to forgive. You have the power to see the moment as something God is using to grow your zeal and focus your passion back on what grows your hunger, significance, and perspective toward Jesus. And that power lies in understanding why you felt offended and then surrendering your unmet expectation to Jesus.

In a practical sense, this looks like forgiving the person, even if they don't believe they were wrong. Forgiveness isn't a choice when you follow Jesus; it's a command. And forgiveness also doesn't mean you have to bring that person or that circumstance back into your life; it means you are choosing to not allow it to pour a foundation of bitterness in your soul, and you're going to see that person or circumstance as an opportunity for growth and love and move on.

When you're walking in the power of the Holy Spirit and at the pace of Jesus, who forgives and sees people in the right way, you're able to see offense for what it is—a corrupter of motives, a polluter of passion, a reservoir of bitterness and frustration. It's a tool the enemy uses to keep you angry for no good reason. Angry enough to forget solitude, angry enough to quit the wilderness trek, and angry enough to forget your identity. Truth is, most offenses are a golden opportunity for you to unpack others' motives and respond with love. It's also a chance to unpack our own motives and realign ourselves to love. And it's how Jesus navigated offense throughout the Gospels—unoffended, focused on loving people, and showing the love of the Father—that gifted us with a path toward wholeness and healing.

IF YOU ARE OFFENDED, UNPACK *THEIR* MOTIVES

We find Jesus mid-ministry preaching up a storm and dealing with people in the only way Jesus knows how—walking at the pace of peace and patience. And it's not that he hasn't dealt with insult or offense; he has. In Matthew 9, we read that Jesus's methods of fasting are questioned by the disciples of John the Baptist, Jesus's cousin and the guy who baptized him and who is now in prison. His disciples are watching and following Jesus to see what he's doing. They see him preach and heal vast numbers of people and yet they ask him, "What's the story with fasting? We fast and the Pharisees fast, but your disciples do not fast!" See, hurting people have a tendency to focus on what you're not doing and miss all the good you are doing. They also bulked themselves up with the religious elite and pretty much said, "You guys are doing this following God thing wrong."

Honestly, questioning Jesus's methods at this point was very offensive, as he is the Son of God. The Son of God whom they, and the disciples of John, probably saw baptized. The same baptism where the heavens opened up, and there were doves and thunder and God's voice spoke: "This is my son, whom I love; with him I am well pleased." Every bit of their questioning was offensive, and Jesus had every right to feel offended and light them on fire verbally. Yet what we see here is that Jesus kept his focus on the path his heavenly Father had laid for him and responded instead with healthy emotions cultivated in the power of the Holy Spirit. He responded with kindness, compassion, and gentleness.

Although he has every right to be offended, Jesus responded with healthy emotions. If you are not responding with Holy Spirit–led emotions, there is a 100 percent chance you have not taken a moment to unpack motives and see the person or circumstance as potentially broken or hurting.

Jesus knew the disciples of John the Baptist weren't motivated by hatred or malice; they were displaced and looking for leadership, as their leader was in prison. Jesus had this innate ability not to get offended, because he was able to unpack motives quickly and with love, and offer peace as a response. And the disciples of John were drowning in emotions, they felt lost, and Jesus, instead of getting offended, answered the question and moved on. His zeal and passion for seeing his Father's will be done were so aligned with his Father's ways and voice that forgiving people's words and assumptions became part of his every day. And we see it again when Jesus healed a man on the Sabbath.

IF YOU ARE OFFENDED, UNPACK *YOUR* MOTIVES

Let me just say that healing anyone on the Sabbath probably felt like giving a middle finger to the religious elite. And

Jesus healed people on the Sabbath several times—not because he was in the business of making religious people angry and walking into holy places with both middle fingers in the air, but because religious people of his day—and still today—will put religious law over walking people toward wholeness every single time. So Jesus was okay that people took offense at the things he did, because he understood their motives as broken and his motives as surrendered passion motivated by his heavenly Father. This does not give you free rein to do what you want and call it Jesus work! The fruit of your life, your words and actions, must align correctly with love and scripture and in a way that brings wholeness and freedom like Jesus did. And Jesus's fruit he was producing was Holy Spirit–led emotions, and healing and wholeness for the masses.

In the Sermon on the Mount, Jesus said, "Along the way, watch out for false prophets. They will come to you in sheep's clothing, but underneath that quaint and innocent wool, they are hungry wolves. *But you will recognize them by their fruits.* You don't find sweet, delicious grapes growing on thorny bushes, do you? You don't find delectable figs growing in the midst of prickly thistles. People and their lives are like trees. Good trees bear beautiful, tasty fruit, but bad trees bear ugly, bitter fruit. A good tree cannot bear ugly, bitter fruit; nor can a bad tree bear fruit that is beautiful and tasty. And what happens to the rotten trees? They are cut down. They are used for firewood. When a prophet comes to you and preaches this or that, *look for his fruits: sweet or sour? rotten or ripe?"* (Matthew 7:15–20 VOICE, emphasis added). And so we find Jesus on the Sabbath walking out a life of good fruit, and in a tussle with thorny religious bushes.

The Sabbath was a day that you weren't allowed to do anything that could have been looked upon as work—which is good, but not when you take something God has instilled for rest and turn it into something religion can use to oppress. In Mark 3, Jesus walks into the synagogue and sees a man with a withered hand. The Pharisees, in all their religious haterade, are watching and waiting for Jesus to say something. These guys aren't just offended; they are plotting to kill Jesus. They haven't even given Jesus a chance. His upbringing offends them. His words and actions offend them; his disciples offend them.

And so in this moment, they were appalled that Jesus would even consider healing this man on the Sabbath, right there in front of everyone! Instead of seeing freedom and wholeness as a good thing, they saw it as offensive, and Jesus, the master unpacker of motives, knew it! Jesus knew their hearts, so he bypassed them and called the man with the withered hand over to him. And then he healed! Like his hand unwithered! What an epic moment. And yet the Pharisees, the religious elite, missed the importance of the miracle and the wholeness brought to this man, because they were offended.

When the Stephanie thing happened, I didn't even take a

moment to unpack my pastor's motives and see the bigger picture, which was that I needed to refocus my passion on Jesus ASAP! But my immaturity and lack of surrendered zeal fueled my motives, which in return offended the whole room. My response was not to see Stephanie as someone with a withered hand Jesus was trying to bring wholeness to; instead she was someone I saw in the way of my calling and gifting! If you are offended, unpack your own emotions. Jesus's motives were to bring wholeness to this man, while the Pharisees' motives were to corner Jesus into doing something they could arrest him for. We will absolutely find ourselves in circumstances where others have corrupted zeal and motives, but we also will find ourselves offended because we too have corrupted zeal and motives.

Also, let me note here that there will be people in our lives who live offended. No matter what we say or do, everything will feel like a middle finger to their establishment. Just respond like Jesus, and make sure your motives are aligned to good fruit that is cultivated in the time spent with the Holy Spirit. Real talk: you can't be the Holy Spirit for people, which means you do not have the power to change hearts and minds. Only Jesus does. The only heart and mind you can change is your own. The only passion you can surrender is your own. The only words you can change are your own. Focus on unpacking your motives. God is big enough to handle everyone else's motives.

IF YOU ARE OFFENDED,
TAKE A MINUTE AND REFOCUS

After all the tussles and potential offenses, Jesus was peopled out and in need of a recharge. Solitude wasn't something he sought once or twice, it was a part of his rhythm, and he knew that to decipher motives and keep his motives pure, he needed time alone. Time with his people. It says in Mark 3:9, after the Sabbath healing, he withdrew with his disciples to the lake to spend time with them and appoint them into ministry. He asked his disciples to have a boat ready to keep the people from crowding him, because everywhere he went the crowds were intense. And everywhere he went, everyone wanted to touch him and get healed. Which, honestly, was invasive and overbearing—as an introvert I would have perceived it as offensive. Like seriously, he needed a minute to just focus on his inner circle. But Jesus understood that when people are desperate, they do desperate things. So he got strategic instead of offended and went away to spend time alone with his twelve friends, not just to hang out but to refocus back on why they were among the people.

He pulled them up that mountain to shift their focus off of all the offensive behavior they'd seen and heard and refocus their hearts back to God and why they were doing what they were doing. Jesus was all about loving the crowds, but he also understood the importance of loving those closest to him. His community was a charging station for him, and that community needed to refocus, as these were the guys who would take his stories and his Father's purpose and plans out to the world when he was gone.

When I was offended by the Stephanie debacle, I didn't reconvene with my community to refocus our hearts and minds on the plans and purpose of God. I huddled with my community to talk crap about poor Stephanie, to say disrespectful things about my pastor's leadership, and to plan for how I was going to make my stand that coming Sunday! I was so focused on being good for the crowds that the fruit I began to produce was toxic. But Jesus, when faced with offense, pulled everyone in to make sure they understood the goal and knew the real purpose of why they were out and about among the people. The goal was love—to be love and produce love. The goal was to bring salvation to the world and restore heaven's purpose for humanity, and they could not do that offended.

When was the last time you got away to recenter your heart and mind on the real goal of this life, which is to love, to be love, and to produce love? When was the last time you pulled your crew in to maybe worship together and pray together, and talk through the struggles you have in a healthy way that builds up instead of tears down? You can't produce good fruit in the soil of offense, and taking time to refocus is like pulling out the weeds that have somehow found their way into your heart and mind. Jesus understood this and needed to make sure everyone was all good, because the next offense would be a doozy!

IF YOU ARE OFFENDED, DON'T ALLOW IT TO CONSUME YOU

I have to be careful with this story, as it's immaturity's favorite Jesus story. It's the story that people who have unhealthy emotions and no accountability like to reference when they offend the room with their truth and zeal. This story isn't an excuse to flip tables; it's a love letter about how to treat people when you are offended.

Jesus had spent most of the early Gospels teaching and healing the sick, but when the Passover festival came around, Jesus headed to the temple. The same sacred space that initiated his hiddenness and growth at twelve had now become a place of swindling those who had come to sacrifice. "When it was almost time for the Jewish Passover, Jesus went up to Jerusalem. In the temple courts he found people selling cattle, sheep and doves, and others sitting at tables exchanging money" (John 2:13–14).

A bit of context. This makeshift flea market wasn't inside the temple; it was in the Court of the Gentiles, which was the outermost courtyard and the only area of the temple where non-Jews were allowed. This court was accessible to the Jews,

Gentiles, foreigners, and the ritually unclean. So these money changers and merchants just set up shop where the unwanted people prayed and congregated. And the money changers, those converting the various currencies to the accepted currency for those needing to pay the temple tax, were cheating people and inflating prices for the people who had traveled from other places to sacrifice and honor God during Passover. They had taken something sacred and corrupted it.

When Jesus sees this space that was set aside for people to pray and instead has been turned into a place where people are being cheated, "he made a whip out of cords, and drove all from the temple courts, both sheep and cattle; he scattered the coins of the money changers and overturned their tables. To those who sold doves he said, 'Get these out of here! Stop turning my Father's house into a market!' His disciples remembered that it is written: 'Zeal for your house will consume me'" (John 2:15–17).

Some of you will get offended and think the right thing to do is to flip the tables of whichever people or establishments have offended you, but if your table flipping doesn't bring healing, you're not working through offense like Jesus did. Jesus in this moment had every reason to be offended. The Matthew account of the temple clearing says after he flipped those tables, "the blind and the lame came to him at the temple, and he healed them" (Matthew 21:14).

Jesus flipped the table, but then he didn't high-five his homies and say, "They had what was coming to them!" Jesus also didn't flip the tables, drop a few F-bombs, and tell the money changers that they suck. Jesus did not go and leave a passive-aggressive tweet or meme or Facebook rant on his platform either. If your righteous anger doesn't have a holy landing point that causes others to be healed and experience God's love, your motives need to be checked. You don't understand broken people's motives, and you need a moment to get away to refocus with people who can keep you accountable.

Jesus didn't flip a table because he was consumed by offense; he flipped a table because he was consumed with zeal for his Father's house. A house that was supposed to be a house of prayer. A house for everyone, regardless of religious affiliation or pedigree. A house for all people to experience heaven on earth. He did this because he was the Yoda of motives and understood how to love people on a deep level.

IF OTHERS ARE OFFENDED, STAY FRAGRANT

After the temple clearing, Jesus continues his speaking tour of sorts, as he knows his ministry and life on earth are coming to an end. He's spending more time speaking about the future and trying to prepare his young disciples for when he is gone. Right after the temple, Judas Iscariot, one of the most famous of Jesus's disciples, makes his bed with the religious elite, and the plot to kill Jesus is in play. We don't really hear a whole lot about Judas until the last few chapters of the Gospels, and when we do hear about him, he's complaining and offended. Jesus, on the other hand, is unbothered and unoffended by the questioning, the religious leaders, and even the money changers he just kicked out of the temple. Nope, Jesus is focused on the plans and purposes God has set before him. And one of the plans of God was to anoint Jesus a few times before his death. And not just with any kind of oil, but with the type of anointing that kings wore. How epic is this? Jesus walks out his final week smelling like royalty; he was going to walk out the worst offenses that he'd ever encountered to date fragrant with the aroma of heaven.

My obsession with smelling nice is a little unhealthy. I have tons of perfumes, and it's not uncommon for people to give me a hug or walk by me and ask me what I'm wearing, or tell me I smell nice. And every single time it happens, I'm reminded of Jesus and all the times in the last week of his life on earth when he was also incredibly fragrant, metaphorically and literally. The life of Jesus gave off heaven vibes, and it was so fragrant people who were near him wanted what he had and followed him from shore to shore. So it's amazing me to see that in Matthew 26 God shows us this beautiful story of Jesus being doused in rare, expensive, and incredibly fragrant oil set apart for royalty. The Son of God now smelled like royalty, and it set him apart from the rest.

The story kicks off with a woman walking over to Jesus

with a year's worth of perfume, and out of love and adoration and honor she pours it over his head. To say this oil was costly would be a vast understatement, but she surrendered all she had, her very best, to Jesus regardless of the cost. Also, her sacrifice offended almost everyone in the room who wasn't fully walking at the pace of peace and filled with the power of the Holy Spirit. And Jesus knew it and allowed it.

Why did he allow it, you might be wondering? Well, because Jesus understood that the fragrance he was wearing was a scent that would follow him in his suffering, in his beating, in the garden, and in the crucifixion. This scent was poured all over his beard, and his hair, and it wasn't something he could just bathe away! It was in his pores. It's the scent of a king that he smelled when he was slapped by the Pharisees during his arrest and the scent of kings that he smelled when he was abandoned. Jesus walked through every betrayal in the last days of his life smelling of royalty, and it was a beautiful reminder to stay focused on God's purpose and plan for him when everyone abandoned him. Jesus, covered in the scent of royalty, remained unoffendable because his life was fragrant with love, peace, joy, patience, and everything in between. This may have been a literal dousing, but his life was covered in the scent of royalty, the fragrance of heaven, even without the physical perfume. And it's how our lives should be lived out as well. If you want to fight off offense, then allow your life to be poured out in worship, all the costly things that could offend the room, lay them at the feet of Jesus, and when struggle comes, that fragrance will keep you focused and moving forward unoffended!

You can't control offense, but you can control living offended. Jesus combated offense by living a fragrant life of sacrifice and love and surrender. If you want to combat offense, you must surrender your zeal to the plan and purpose of God the way Jesus did. This allows you to see people's motives and respond with love. It also allows you a deep dive into your motives and time that refocuses your heart and mind toward love. It also keeps your zeal producing the right fruit that's consumed with the right thing. If you are easily offended, check what you are passionate about and entrusted with and ask yourself, have I fully surrendered this task or person or passion to God? If you haven't, do it today. Because if you don't, the offense will find you and produce anger, bitterness, and Judas tendencies.

Forgive.

Ask for forgiveness.

Be nice to Stephanie.

Surrender your zeal.

Unpack motives—yours, theirs, everyone's.

Stay fragrant.

Not everyone is out to betray you.

Onward.

CHAPTER 8
HIS DISCRETION

How to deal with feeling betrayed

**Betrayal is like a knife wound:
only possible up close.**

There are countless moments in my life when I have felt betrayed—or what I like to call *aggressively deceived*. You know the feeling. It's when someone you love dearly or hold in high esteem, who has access to your life and heart, stabs you with their words or actions. In response, you tend to feel like trust has been severed in a way that is irreparable and, at times, trauma-inducing. I've come to call the feelings associated with betrayal, the feelings that only come from the treachery that stabs you up close and personal, a deceiving of time and love and trust. That is what betrayal is, after all: a breach of trust or disloyalty with words or actions. And if you are a part of humanity, you have had to navigate this in your relationships, in your life and jobs, and in more ways than one.

What I have learned over time is that there are usually three types of betrayal: betrayal experienced due to our own immaturity, betrayal experienced due to others' immaturity, and betrayal experienced because of those who are offended. Whichever way you've encountered betrayal, what I've found is that regardless of how it comes at you, it always shifts how you see people moving forward as well as in your faith walk. You don't want your perspective on how to love people and how to follow Jesus to be corrupted by betrayal, as loving people and loving God well is really our one job. I've experienced personal breaches of trust by friends and leaders, and in various relationships, but my greatest betrayals have been caused by my own personal immaturity and inability to see circumstances and people the way God sees them. This has kept me from knowing what God is really doing and trying to grow in me. And I have no one to blame but myself.

In my early twenties, I was offered a position working for a youth program that helped teens in drug rehab. This wasn't just a rehab center; it was a center for kids who also had extensive and violent criminal records. I had reservations, but they said my job was to help the schoolteachers during the school day and grade papers. It felt easy enough, and it felt purposeful. So many of these kids had stories that were heartbreaking, but to be honest, most were just incredibly scary. But I was young and naïve, and I believed if I could just love them like Jesus does, that would be all they needed to change.

In the first few months, everything seemed amazing, although I was warned that there would be violent moments and I needed to be careful with the kids. I didn't think anything of it because I was twenty-two years old, and I just saw them as teenagers in my youth group. I was also asked on several occasions not to assume these kids were my friends or let them call me by my first name. But I did anyway, and I just chalked up the warning to older people not understanding how cool I was with the kids. Also, these were not kids; they were seventeen years old, almost adults, and most had massive criminal records for assault and everything else you could imagine. They'd lived way more life than I could have ever imagined, but in my youth I assumed I was really thriving when for sure I was not.

I don't want to make excuses for what happened next, but I will say that I was super new to this atmosphere and contending with the level of emotional trauma these kids had endured. I'd only ever worked in vocational ministry and with young children. Looking back now, I can see my immaturity betrayed my perspective and my ability to see the circumstances as dangerous. It also told me I was up for the challenge of helping with this level of brokenness. But I was not.

On one random Thursday, a massive fight broke out in the classroom. I mean, chairs and desks were thrown, and faces were bloodied. It felt like a real-life prison fight, and I was the only staff member in the room close enough to stop it. I tried to break it up when Billy (not his real name), one of the gang leaders at this rehab center and a kid I'd been kind to, pushed me backward away from the fight and then aggressively pushed me into an office and shielded me from a potential assault until security came to break things up.

This incident changed how I saw people, and not in a good way. I'd spent six months at that center believing I was building mentor-like relationships with Billy and a whole slew of teens, but I wasn't. Their focus was their mental health, not my safety or validating my desire to be liked, admired, or looked up to. Even though I spent time trying to pray with them and encouraging them in their faith and life, which wasn't allowed, the whole time I didn't realize what room I was in. I was unable to see the truth in the situation due to my lack of spiritual and emotional maturity. And the truth was, I had no idea what I was doing. I trusted what I thought was my faith and my horrible early ministry training. But I was not prepared for this level of trauma.

When you're surrounded by brokenness, you have to know how to speak, how to respond, how to walk away, and how to let go. If not, your immaturity will tell you other people's brokenness betrayed you, when the reality is you were in the wrong room. Most betrayals will be experienced when you navigate dealing with immature people, offensive circumstances, and their lack of discretion to know how you should respond. But in this scenario, I was unable to read the room, and I didn't know how to respond to people, especially hurting people trying to navigate their own personal brokenness.

I'm not blaming myself for the incident or for their actions, although my inability to understand the teens I was dealing with and see the circumstance as unsafe opened the moment for violence because they knew I didn't have any idea how to help or whom to call. My tenure was spent trying to be cool with the teens instead of really learning about them and how to help them. And so I do hold myself responsible for putting myself in an unsafe situation and for not listening to my training and the warnings that I was given daily by the older teachers who had been in that environment for years. I believed these kids were my friends and would never put me in a situation that could harm me, and after that incident, I felt betrayed by them. The chairs flying through the room were harmful and scary. But the one who betrayed me was me. I shouldn't have let the kids call me by my first name. I thought I was cool and edgy and making the students like me. But what I did was unknowingly remove the thing that made the kids realize I was an authority figure and not their peer. I also showed up to work in streetwear instead of professional clothing. The school had given us a dress code that I broke daily. My youth and immaturity told me to dress fun and approachable, and now, looking back, I can see what I was doing was saying to those watching that, like the students, I didn't respect the establishment.

All I wanted was the kids to see Jesus in the way that I lived and loved and served them. But they saw I was a fake peer and someone who didn't warrant respect because I hadn't modeled respect for people either. Betrayal is like a knife wound: only possible up close. And in this scenario, as scary as it was, and even though I felt betrayed by the kids I had tried to help, the one who betrayed me the most in this situation was my inability to read the room. My inability to assess the situation and see true motives failed me here. My immaturity to see the job as a job betrayed me. And as much as I could blame other people for this moment, it was me who betrayed my safety in this scenario. I just didn't realize it until many years later.

LEARN TO READ THE ROOM

Reading the room takes maturity. It's the ability to walk into a situation knowing what God is doing and then what you should be doing in return. It keeps you focused on people the way Jesus focused on people; it keeps you aware and full of wisdom so you can deal with people well and with love. Betrayal tends to lurk in the hearts of those who can't read the room, because if you don't know what God is doing in your midst or if you lose trust that he is at work on your behalf, you will turn to feel betrayed by people and circumstances.

Betrayal, the absolute breach of trust, is only able to attack your emotions when they aren't fully rooted in whatever God is doing. Jesus was fully focused on his heavenly Father's plan, so he was unoffendable. Even though people committed horrible acts of betrayal, Jesus only saw them as hurting people in need of a savior. And he did this because he was always reading the room. Reading the room means you can see the people who need you in the sea of those who don't. Reading the room means you know how to lovingly bypass the people you have no business giving time and trust to. When I'm reading the room, it helps me navigate possible situations where people might betray my trust.

In my youth, I brought everyone close, like I did with these students. I trusted everyone who showed me kindness, and I allowed everyone to know everything about me and my dreams. And then, when people didn't handle my heart and dreams with care, I felt betrayed. But twenty-plus years of ministry and forty-plus years of life have now taught me that to fight off betrayal by people and circumstances, you need to learn how to read the room, because your immaturity is not trustworthy, and it will walk you into a space you have no business being in, and right past the people and growth opportunities you're really meant to invest in.

Reading the room gives your heart a moment to assess whether the room you want to go inside and the people who are there are trustworthy, and whether they are moving at the pace of Jesus. Not everyone has earned the right to your time and trust, and Jesus modeled how to guard our hearts, because guarding your heart and your time doesn't make you mean; it makes you wise and purposeful and free from feeling betrayed. It helps keep you out of the wrong fights, jobs, relationships, and emotions. We see this lived out in the early chapters of Mark, when a man named Jairus approached Jesus because his daughter was sick, and he asked Jesus to come with him and heal his daughter. Jesus is awesome and says yes and heads toward this man's home. But as he walks there, it's awkwardly packed. Jesus is there, his disciples are there, the dad is there, and a massive crowd is following them.

Jesus is walking, being pushed by the crowd, which is full of people with agendas and real-life needs, and then he stops. He stops because he has felt someone touch him and power leave his body. Guys, everyone was touching him and pressed against him, and when he asks who it was that reached out to him, some of the disciples huff and puff about having to stop and try to explain to Jesus that no one touched him. Immaturity will betray you and tell you to move on, to bypass people, and tell Jesus what he should do. Finally, fearful and trembling, a woman spoke up and said she was indeed the one who touched him. We find out this is a woman who has had a period for like twelve years. She is desperate for healing and is shunned by society, and she has pressed through the crowd (which probably would have stoned her if they realized she was there, because she was ceremonially unclean) to get to him. Jesus is so aware of his emotional and spiritual state that when she touches him, he stops, and she gets her healing. It's epic. And it happened because Jesus, in the middle of the commotion, other people's emotions and expectations, was able to read the room and see the need.

When I worked at that rehab center, I assumed my way of ministering to hurting people was the best way. Yet Jesus sent mature people to guide me over those months. My immaturity scoffed, tried to move them along, and I didn't listen. But when this happened to Jesus, he cleared the bench.

Jesus has just healed this woman, and he is speaking to her, when someone walks up and interrupts to tell him the girl they were going to see has died. It's a bit of a mess, as you can just imagine. Emotions are heightened, and then Jesus assesses the hearts of the people and the severity of the moment and tells everyone they are not permitted to follow him. He moves on with just Peter, James, and John on the next leg of this journey. Jesus was about to walk into a very emotional situation, and you know what he didn't need? More emotional people who don't know how to read the room! Jesus arrived, people are screaming and wailing—it was a hot mess. So he goes into the house with just the people he brought, and guess what? The girl is healed, *bing bang boom*, another miracle. But it didn't happen with everyone there watching.

It wasn't even with all his disciples. It was with his inner circle.

Jesus understood that if you live your life trying to make everyone happy, you'll not only be the receiver of a load of betrayal, but you will betray the expectations of everyone who hasn't earned the right to you. And at this moment, he read the room, and his focus was on the sick girl and not on all the immature people following, waiting for an Instagram moment. Jesus was always keenly aware of the people he was loving and leading, and so he was able to bypass feeling misunderstood, or feeling like others didn't understand his motives. My focus in the classroom with the teens was making sure they liked me. Jesus in this scenario was about following the will of his heavenly Father. I betrayed myself and the teachers who trusted me to carry out their rules and ways. Jesus read the room, loved people along the way, and made sure his Father's purpose of wholeness was what people experienced when they encountered him.

Jesus's unhurried pace kept him focused on his Father's will. His unhurried pace allowed Jesus to read the room. And it's Jesus who should be our guide on who to invest our words and our time in. Betrayal will always find a way into our hearts when we believe we are misunderstood in the room, or when our words fall on deaf ears in the room. Truth is, you are the only person who can allow betrayal to infiltrate your life. It's a bit like offense. You can't stop people from failing you, but you can choose to read the room, understand their motives, and move forward with those who understand the moments. Learn how to read the room, as it will keep your heart free from feeling betrayed by immaturity and misunderstanding. Let Jesus's unrushed and unbothered pace allow you to take in the right advice and truly assess the room's level of trust. Immaturity will tell you that you don't need to read the room and that you need to just move it along, but if you don't pause and assess, you'll end up like Peter, always in a rush, always speaking out of turn and cutting people's ears off.

LEARN TO LISTEN

Peter is one of my favorite characters in the Bible, and he also famously betrayed Jesus not once but three times. Peter also consistently showed his immaturity and outspoken passion, which violated Jesus's trust and caused Jesus to call him out and rebuke him in public.

In Matthew 17, we see what's known as the Transfiguration. Jesus has a beautiful moment with his inner circle, where he takes them up a mountainside, and Moses and Elijah show up and start talking to Jesus. It's one of those "just be silent and watch" moments, yet Peter decides to chime in and say, "Lord, it is good for us to be here." Jesus's secondhand embarrassment must have been massive! He then goes on: "If you wish, I will put up three shelters—one for you, one for Moses and one for Elijah." And as he is talking, **God the Father cuts him**

off with "This is my Son, whom I love; with him I am well pleased. Listen to him." Do you know what it is to be cut off mid-sentence by the creator of the world? I can't even imagine. Listening isn't an ear thing, it's a heart thing, and Peter was hearing what was going on, but he wasn't really listening to what was happening.

Peter exhibits this kind of immature behavior again in Mark 8, when Jesus begins to explain to his disciples that he will have to suffer many things and he will be killed, but not to worry as in three days he will rise up. And good ol' immature Peter doesn't listen. Peter takes Jesus aside and rebukes him. Jesus, in response to this immaturity, says, "Get behind me, Satan!...You do not have in mind the concerns of God, but merely human concerns." Jesus called him Satan and told him to get back on his pace.

I'm not being harsh by saying Peter's immaturity and inability to listen led to moments of betrayal. Betrayal doesn't just happen. People don't wake up one morning and say, "I'm going to cheat on my spouse today." It's gradual, it's granular, and it happens over time. And Peter's lack of discretion and immaturity kept him moving toward not only a betrayal of words but a betrayal of action. We see his stumbles escalate when Peter famously backtalks Jesus at the Last Supper in Luke 22. We see Jesus trying to work through his last moments with his disciples; he's unpacking the kingdom and what is to come for them in the future, and enter Peter:

Peter: Lord, what are You talking about? I'm going all the way to the end with You—to prison, to execution—I'm prepared to do anything for You.

Jesus: No, Peter, the truth is that before the rooster crows at dawn, you will have denied that you even know Me, not just once, but three times (Luke 22:33–34 VOICE).

And Jesus was not wrong. Peter did exactly what Jesus said. After Jesus's arrest, he denied Jesus three times. And yet Jesus did not get rid of Peter. He kept him around, teaching him, loving him, and eventually restoring him.

Listen closely. Jesus models how to navigate betrayal by immaturity right here, through his interactions with the apostle Peter. Jesus didn't get rid of Peter; he pulled him closer. Jesus didn't rebuke Peter and never speak to him again; no, he corrected him on what to say and how to perceive circumstances with discretion. Jesus didn't tell Peter "I told you so" when he denied him for the third time. The Bible says he glanced over at Peter and made eye contact with him, the same eye contact that told Peter to just listen on the mountain of transfiguration, the same look he gave him when Peter spoke out of turn, and the same look he gave Peter when Peter said, "I'm going all the way to the end with you—to prison, to execution—I'm prepared to do anything for you." Jesus's response to betrayal was to use the betrayal as teachable moments. Moments to pull closer, to show forgiveness, and ultimately to restore. Jesus was invested in Peter, and he wanted to see him win, even if it meant he had to deal with some very blatant disrespect that would eventually betray him.

Peter didn't know how to read the room or listen, so he lived those early years unknowingly betraying Jesus. Jesus read the room and was always listening, to his Father, to his disciples, and to people who were stretching out to touch him in the middle of a crowd. And Jesus's ability to listen and really hear what is going on caused him to respond with love.

That's how we should respond when we feel like trust has been breached. First, we need to assess the room. What is God doing? He is always moving and growing someone or something! Is this circumstance or the person who betrayed me something or someone I can still bring closer? Is this a teaching moment? Is this person just immature? They won't always be immature, but if you throw someone away because they don't know better, you could be throwing away someone like Peter. The same Peter who ended up helping change the world.

LEARN TO LET GO

Offended people will throw you under a bus of betrayal and then put that bus in reverse and run you over again! And Judas Iscariot was this level of offended. He did not care about reading a room and seeing what God was doing! He didn't care to listen to see what Jesus said, because whatever had offended him made him deaf to Jesus's thoughts and ideas and pace. Judas was one of Jesus's original twelve disciples, and is such a part of the inner circle that he is entrusted with the money. He has a vested interest in what the disciples do, where they go, and how they spend the money, as it's well known among the disciples that Judas has been taking money from the group. We see this when Jesus, during his last week, is being anointed by a costly fragrance.

> Judas Iscariot, one of his disciples (who was plotting to betray Jesus), began to speak.
>
> **Judas Iscariot:** How could she pour out this vast amount of fine oil? Why didn't she sell it? It is worth nearly a year's wages; the money could have been given to the poor.
>
> This had nothing to do with Judas's desire to help the poor. The truth is he served as the treasurer, and he helped himself to the money from the common pot at every opportunity. (John 12:4–6 VOICE)

Betrayal with a side of offense will cause you to see all the good stuff God is doing in your life as offensive and a waste of time. But Jesus didn't allow this level of offense and potential betrayal to stall his purpose or affect his pace; he continued to love Judas, knowing full well Judas would be responsible for his arrest and death. He spoke purpose over Judas in the midst of Judas betraying him.

In Matthew 26, Jesus sees the soldiers approaching. Judas kisses Jesus to show the soldiers which one he is. And yet in all the translations, Jesus calls Judas friend in this moment and asks him why he has come. Actually, the word Jesus uses translates to "comrade," a partner in arms! Even as he was being betrayed, Jesus was speaking purpose over Judas. He was reminding Judas that he was purposed for more than the betrayal.

If you want to fight off betrayal based on immaturity, listen to the person who is hurting you. Take time to teach them, rebuke them if needed, and make sure to listen to what God says about them. And then give the look and make sure to restore them.

But if you're facing a Judas, the kind of betrayal that is deliberate and hateful and is trying to kill something you love or believe in, forgive them, and if given the moment, remind them who they are. Jesus didn't rebuke Judas like he did Peter. Judas betrayed Jesus because he was offended, not because he was immature. Judas was one of those always offended by something, but mainly when money was on the table. He was super offended by the woman who poured out the oil on Jesus. He wanted the oil so he could cash it in as he was the treasurer of the group and pocketing money for himself. You can read this tea in the book of John, chapter 12 (ESV):

But Judas Iscariot, one of his disciples (he who was about to betray him), said, "Why was this ointment not sold for three hundred denarii and given to the poor?" He said this, not because he cared about the poor, but because he was a thief, and having charge of the moneybag he used to help himself to what was put into it.

And Jesus knew when people are offended, you have to bring them back to why they're in the room. He had to bring Judas back to purpose and then let him go. Not every relationship that has experienced betrayal will be restored, and not every relationship can be fixed like his relationship with Peter. Some will end like Judas. But make sure when you let the people go, you let them go with forgiveness and purpose, as Jesus was not in the business of leaving people torn down but built up. Forgiveness is a major antidote to living in the bitterness of betrayal.

LEARN TO STAY FOCUSED

Then, in Matthew 27, Jesus comes face-to-face with the religious elite, and the plot to execute him is in place. They've been yelling at him, falsely accusing him of things, and beating him for hours, and all Jesus's friends have abandoned him. He is in a bucket of betrayal, listening to his Father's voice, and letting go of the things these people are saying to him in order to keep his heart focused on the goal ahead: the goal to redeem heaven's initial plan for humanity. Jesus has every reason to feel overwhelmed, lonely, fearful, unsafe, insecure, anxious, and heavily offended and betrayed. But he does not. Even when he's brought in front of Pilate, the governor who could save his life, Jesus doesn't pick a fight. He doesn't plead for mercy; he responds with patience in the process and plans his heavenly Father has put in place. Again, unbothered by earthly and temporal circumstances, Jesus embraces whatever is to come, as he is so connected to

his Father's voice,

his Father's presence,

his Father's words,

his Father's ways,

his Father's point of view,

his Father's pace,

his Father's motives,

and his Father's discretion.

All these things are helping him stay focused on the freedom that will be experienced by all if he stays the course.

In the next few verses, Jesus is stripped naked and beaten until he is unrecognizable. The Pharisees and Romans didn't just mean to execute him via crucifixion; they meant to embarrass him and remove any semblance of the man he appeared to be. When they were done beating him to the point almost of death, they flipped him around and did it again. And just when Jesus could barely take any more, they strapped half of his cross to his back and made him walk to the execution site. Thankfully, there was a man who helped carry the cross because, at that point, Jesus was barely holding on.

In Matthew 27:32–44 we find Jesus nailed to the cross and suffocating. Crucifixion was the worst imaginable death at the time. And yet Jesus, hanging on the cross, beaten by the Pharisees, flogged by the Romans, and abandoned by his friends and followers, used his final breaths to be love and show love to those nailed to the cross next to him. He kept the purpose and plans of his heavenly Father moving, even in the treachery of his friends and followers; Jesus kept the pace of peace even on the cross, even in the betrayal.

When you feel the most betrayed, do you stay focused and reflect love? Do you remind people who are offended and immature that they have a purpose and that the door is always open for reconciliation? It's okay if you haven't, but now you know how to respond, and we are all now accountable to it. Accountable for being love and producing love even when we are met with a level of unfairness that feels like crucifixion, humiliation, and repeated flogging.

Jesus had every reason to feel betrayed and unleash a very well-deserved retaliation on humanity, but instead, as he headed toward his last moments, with perspective on his lips, "Eli, Eli, lema sabachthani?" (My God, my God, why have you forsaken me?). Some would read this and assume he now felt betrayed by his heavenly Father; I know I did in my first passing of the passage. But Jesus didn't suddenly halt his pace; he used the diminishing strength he had to quote scripture. "My God, my God, why have you forsaken me?" This plea to the Father is the very first line in Psalm 22. Jesus, dying on the cross, abandoned and betrayed, went back to quoting scripture. Anyone who knew the scriptures would have immediately known what he was saying, and it was powerful. What he had done in hiddenness and again in the wilderness, he was repeating on the cross. He was reaching toward his heavenly Father and activating the power of the Holy Spirit from the very pit of his reservoir of peace to remind himself in the agony and betrayal that his Father still had a plan and purpose for his life. He was shifting his perspective to the holiness of his Father, who was enthroned above all heaven and earth. He was calling out to him and letting him know that even in this horrible moment, he knew God was still God, and God was still good.

What would the world look like if we, as followers of Jesus, didn't abandon the ways of Jesus when life got hard? What if instead, we read the room to see what God was doing when our emotions and immaturity betrayed us? What would our lives look like if we walked the earth like Jesus, unbothered and always prepared to see someone healed? Even if it was offensive to stop. Even if others' expectations had to be thrown out the window. What would life look like if the Peters of the world had a safe place to become everything they were called to be because we weren't quick to feel betrayed by their immaturity? How healthy would our emotions be if we looked at the Judases of the world and, instead of telling them how horrible they are, we spoke purpose and lovingly let them go?

It seems too vast a request, so I'll just ask, what if just you and I did this? What kind of ripple would we cause? What if when betrayal laced with offense came our way, we responded with kindness? What if when betrayal laced with immaturity made another mistake, we stayed silent and instead shot over a kind glance and patiently reminded the person that it's okay, they have another chance to be better? Gosh, what would happen to our lives and our world if when we felt the most beaten down and the most crucified by unfairness, we responded in love and spoke life?

Let's be honest: life will never be betrayal-free. You will feel and be betrayed at some point, but Jesus mapped out how to respond. Even when it's you that is betraying yourself with your own pace and perspective and emotions, love is always the key to responding.

Sometimes you may just have to remind yourself that you are indeed a friend of Jesus, and perhaps you may have to stare yourself down in a mirror just to remind yourself that you know better and can be better. Other times it will mean remaining silent or giving a loving response in the midst of crucifixion.

No matter what kind of betrayal you encounter:
Always read the room.
Keep your ears and heart open for restoration.
Always push people back to purpose.
Stay focused on the scriptures.
It's okay to be disappointed.
Onward.

CHAPTER 9
HIS PERSPECTIVE

How to deal with feeling disappointed

**The struggle is not a setback;
it's a setup. View it wisely.**

I am covered in physical scars from wounds I didn't see coming. Scars from random childhood hiccups, like letting go
of the treadmill handle when I was five while it was going full
speed, which then caused me to go flying backward into a
glass credenza. I have scars from trying to love a cat that didn't
love me back. I have a scar above my left eye from the time I

was knocked unconscious by a vacuum cleaner. I was trying to leave work early, and I was rushing through the process of cleaning and haphazardly vacuumed over a piece of metal that then violently jumped up and hit me and caused my knees to buckle. I then fell on top of the vacuum cord, which then shot out of the wall like a missile and hit me in the nose. I saw stars and then everything faded to black. I can't make this stuff up!

I have a scar under my left eye from a canoeing accident at church camp—and by canoeing accident, I mean I got knocked unconscious with a paddle.

Wounds from unforeseen disappointments and mundane circumstances seem to be a major theme in my life. I have a scar on my wrist from breaking a glass window by accident. I had locked myself out of my house and tried to finagle my way through a small window. The window was not having it and broke—with me in it! It wasn't pretty. Then there's the scar on my knee from jumping out of a moving car I was driving because I saw a spider on the windshield, and I panicked.

I am also covered in emotional scars no one sees, from wounds no one realized I had. These emotional scars, like my physical ones, have been collected over years of navigating funny and not-so-funny circumstances and people I cared about who disappointed me. Scars from past relationships, friendships, and dreams unrealized. Most of my emotional scars are healed and barely noticeable, and others are still very visible in my words and in moments when I stop moving at the pace of Jesus, when I stop responding in love, and when

I'm hurried and offended and not fully focused on God's plans and purposes for my life. And what I've learned over the years is that disappointment has been the major culprit behind the scars in my life: moments when I thought things were going to go one way, and then they took a quick left turn and left me with sadness and unmet hopes and expectations. Especially that car one, as spiders are the devil, and my car hit another car, and I got a $467 ticket because the entire thing unfolded in front of a policeman parked across the street! True story.

But regardless of how much disappointment you have faced or what wounds caused our emotional and physical scars, each moment is a road map in our lives. Some represent disappointments God used to help mature me or storms that strengthened me. But each scar has the potential to build our perspective in the middle of a wound or mishap. Each scar, if you allow it, can teach you a lesson about God's faithfulness. Each of my now-healed wounds is a reminder of lessons I honestly don't ever want to have to learn again. But I love and embrace my scars and disappointments, physical and emotional, because they have helped me become the woman I am.

My mistakes and disappointments have fashioned the way I friend and follow Jesus and who I am as a human. Sadly, what I have found in loving and serving people through their disappointments is that most of us miss the lesson that can be found in what we perceive as a setback. As a result, we resent the scar and miss out on the lesson. But if we embrace the disappointments in our lives the way Jesus faced his, I guarantee that what we will find are life lessons that will equip us for whatever disappointment tries to throw our emotions through a glass credenza. We just need to change how we see the frustrations while we are in it. We need a fresh perspective.

You may find physical and emotional scars to be ugly or triggering, but I have chosen to see mine as beautiful reminders of God's hand in my life. And yes, some are still triggering, but when I feel the unhealthy emotions bubbling up to remind me of the struggle I've already worked and walked through, I remember the pace of peace. I reach for the Holy Spirit perspective found in Jesus, which cultivates good emotions, and I will myself to see a lesson in the struggle. Watching adults navigate marriages when I was young taught me the kind of husband I wanted and the kind of wife I wanted to be. The failures within my friendships showed me the kind of people I should bring close and the kind of friend I wanted to be. Every time I had a professional struggle, I made it a point to note what worked and what did not; I didn't want to repeat the patterns of struggle or disappointment. I made it a point to learn everything I could in the struggle and disappointment, as I never wanted to unleash my wounds and the eventual scars people had unleashed on other people and on me. And thankfully, even though I faced countless disappointments and unmet expectations, my scars taught me what kind of follower of Jesus I wanted to be, and it always led me back to Jesus. Everything, even disappointment, has the power to teach you something; you just have to choose to see disappointment the way Jesus viewed it. And Jesus viewed it as an opportunity for growth.

Now imagine me holding your shoulders and looking into the whites of your eyes like your intense Cuban auntie for this next part. If you have made it this deep into this emotional roller coaster of a book, first of all, I love you, and good job! Second, don't miss this perspective-shifting life hack that took me tons of years and emotional and physical scars to finally work out. Life will look really different for you if you can filter your disappointments through a heavenly, Jesus-like viewpoint that sees disappointment as an opportunity. I'm talking about embracing the type of perspective that shifts our hearts and minds to experience love, joy, and peace in the crying in the corners moments. But you can't see an opportunity for growth if you never assess the wound of disappointment like Jesus did.

IF YOU FEEL WOUNDED BY DISAPPOINTMENT, ASSESS THE WOUND

If you are human, with a heart and feelings, you'll be disappointed. But when we do find ourselves disappointed, we need to check the wound, as wounds, like disappointment, won't just heal on their own. Wounds caused by disappointment will fester and get infected, and then they can fill you with things like bitterness, sadness, hopelessness, fear, loneliness, and everything else you don't want to sit in. So when facing unmet expectations or disappointment, it's good to check your wounds and assess what kind of help you need. For some, it will be a very well-placed therapy appointment to process the wound, and that is perfectly okay. But when Jesus felt disappointed and wounded by those he loved, he didn't have a tele-doc he could schedule a call with. He had the voice of his heavenly Father, the presence of the Holy Spirit, and a bunch of disciples/friends who were super disappointing. This feels relatable to me, on a deep level.

We see how Jesus responds to disappointment right after Judas kisses him and the soldiers begin to arrest him. Peter, in the tussle and confusion, pulls out a sword and cuts off one of the ears of the guys in the arresting mob! We see this unfold in Luke 22. Everyone is working out how to navigate the major wound of disappointment they are about to get handed, especially Jesus.

Disciples (*realizing what was going on*): Lord, is this why You told us to bring the swords? Should we attack?

Before Jesus could answer, one of them had swung his sword at the high priest's slave, cutting off his right ear.

Jesus: Stop! No more of this!

Then He reached out to touch—and heal—the man's ear. Jesus turned to the chief priests, the captains of the temple, and the elders and spoke.

Jesus: Do you think I'm some sort of violent criminal? Is that why you came with swords and clubs? I haven't been hard to find—each day I've been in the temple in broad daylight, and you never tried to seize Me there. But this is your time—night—and this is your power— the power of darkness.

They grabbed Him at this point and took Him away to the high priest's home. Peter followed—at a distance. (Luke 22:49–54 VOICE)

Nothing could be more disappointing or wounding than teaching someone to do something that they repeatedly fail at. Jesus loved and taught and showed his disciples in vivid detail how to respond to people's various levels of brokenness in a healthy way. And then, when things got tough, they folded under pressure. Not because they were bad people, but because they were super young and immature. Jesus was aware of their failures, and even though it was disappointing, even though it wounded him, he kept things moving forward toward his heavenly Father's plan with kindness and perspective.

Also, for clarity, Jesus never told his disciples to bring swords to the garden; he told them things were going to get difficult, and these dum-dums assumed swords were the answer—what a face-palm moment for Jesus. I sometimes wonder whether, when everything was happening, and the disciples were standing around asking about swords, and Peter cut someone's ear off, Jesus gave him a look. I wonder if, when Jesus bent down and picked up the guy's ear off the ground and reattached it, he was staring them down like, "For real?" But what we see is not a look of disdain but the ability to assess that, yes, this was a super disappointing moment. And the right solution for this current wound of disappointment was to de-escalate with strength rooted in kindness and facts over feelings.

IF YOU FEEL WOUNDED BY DISAPPOINTMENT, CAUTERIZE THE BLEEDING

You know what you don't want to do when you are wounded by disappointment? Get all in your feelings and bleed out. You want to de-escalate the situation with a healthy perspective that engages healthy emotions like kindness, compassion, patience, and peace. Jesus was able to see that these kids were just super immature, and this moment was legit scary and overwhelming. He also saw that these people there to arrest him had horrible motives. From the weapons they brought to the time of night they came, it was all screaming, "DIS-APPOINTMENT." But Jesus didn't let the wound from his disciples' failure or the arrest fester. He bent down and healed a man's ear! There are miracles and people whom you can help in the middle of your disappointment. You just must be mature enough, and attached to peace in such a way, that you can see past your feelings in the moment.

Have you ever encountered someone explaining their wound, but all you get is their feelings about what happened and not the facts? Jesus cut right through their feelings and went directly to the facts.

Fact: the disciples were young and immature.

Fact: those coming to arrest Jesus were motivated by greed, and blatantly wrong.

Fact: even in the disappointment, God was still good and in control.

When life throws disappointment at you, assess the wound and cauterize the bleeding with facts over feelings. It will hurt, but it will stop the wound from getting infected and keep you moving forward. Jesus didn't have time to sit in his feelings and feel offended, betrayed, and disappointed. He had a tough night ahead, and he needed all his feelings tapped into his Father's voice and presence to navigate the struggle that he was about to face.

When you focus on the facts of a situation over your feelings about the situation, you're able to direct your feeling in a healthy way. Sometimes this means I'll go back to an email or text conversation and read it out loud to someone I trust, which is usually my levelheaded husband, and ask what I'm missing. I bring in people who are far enough from this situation that has sucker-punched my expectations and caused me to unravel in my feelings to help me navigate it with facts. You know who I don't bring in? That person who is always down for a good fight and will make my feelings louder than the facts. Because if I do that, I will turn into the "reap what you sow" lady.

Sadly, when faced with people and disappointments, most of us feel like there has been some major injustice that we've now been subjected to. When you are led by your feelings after disappointment, you'll hope whoever or whatever hurt you will get theirs in the end, and some of us who have been in church too long say things like, "They will reap what they've sown!" Have you ever watched someone reap what they have sown? I have, and it's horrible! That is the opposite of what you want. I'm not saying stop hoping for and believing in justice, but if restoration is possible, wouldn't we want that first? Shouldn't we believe in and hope for people and disappointments to unravel and be restored? Shouldn't we bend down and heal ears in the fights and struggles? That's what Jesus did, and that's how I want to navigate disappointing people and circumstances as well. It doesn't mean I'm going to be best friends with Judas or have brunch with the ear guy; it just means I am certain that God is still good, God is still in control, and I will keep moving toward the facts about God's plan instead of my feelings in the moment.

Jesus's life modeled how to be laser-focused on the purpose and plans his heavenly Father had for him, even while facing disappointment. And he did it by understanding that yes, disappointment can wound, but we have the maturity to assess the wound and the Holy Spirit wherewithal to stop the bleeding. He had this type of triage perspective long before his arrest. He had that focus at age twelve, in the temple, when he stepped back into hiddenness, and then again, that perspective helped him see the cross as another entryway to hiddenness. He knew because he'd experienced hiddenness before that only good things were to come from any form of hiddenness. But the world around him didn't see what Jesus saw; all they saw were feelings, and all they felt were sadness and disappointment. And they took Jesus's arrest and eventual death on the cross as a setback instead of an eternal setup.

IF YOU FEEL WOUNDED BY DISAPPOINTMENT, DON'T PULL THE STITCHES

One of my largest scars is under my chin. I got this scar when I was seven, because I was running full speed in my cousin's kitchen in my socks and tripped and flew face-first into the tile. My uncle immediately saw the slide, knew it was bad, and grabbed my face to stop the bleeding. He then took me to the home of a family member who was a doctor to sew my face closed. Everything was on the mend and all good until, in my immaturity and curiosity, I pulled out the stitches too early! The wound wasn't fully healed, and I made a mess, and now I have a gnarly scar to remind me of the wound.

Sometimes the greatest thing you can do when you are drowning in disappointment is to allow the moment to play out. I can't tell you how many emotional wounds and disappointments I didn't give time to play out or heal. I either didn't assess the wound's severity, or didn't stop the emotional bleeding well enough, and I pulled the stitches out way too early! Jesus never pulled the stitches out early. If there was a moment of unmet expectations or hopelessness, he paused, assessed, and responded with patience. He lived in the beautiful trust and unhurried peace that walked him through every bit of his feelings and the last hours of his earthly life.

We see this play out when Jesus gets arrested in the garden, unfairly and illegally. Yet he allows it. It's frustrating and sad, and all his disciples abandon him, except Peter, who we have already witnessed isn't good in bad situations. Jesus is now facing the religious elite, who hate him and who beat him and question him throughout the night in secret. There is no help coming for Jesus, as during the night, Peter denies him three times and then runs off in his feelings and leaves Jesus behind. And as the sun rises, Judas realizes what he's done, becomes remorseful, and tells the chief priests and elders that Jesus is innocent, and he has betrayed an innocent man. It's one big, gigantic bowl of disappointment, because Judas, ironically the only person who speaks to Jesus's innocence, then runs off and ends his life. And though we see a hopeless scenario, Jesus sees an opportunity for heaven's plan to unfold on the earth, and Jesus remains steadfast, unmovable, strong, and full of peace.

Jesus is then taken in front of the governor under false pretenses. And even though Pilate could save Jesus from this mess, he instead washes his hands of this horrifying situation. Nothing is more disappointing than facing an unfair circumstance and having someone in leadership who can help choose not to get involved. It feels wrong and drenched in injustice and frustration. And then, after a long night of indictments against Jesus that were false and unproven, Jesus faces the people he healed, loved, and flipped tables for. He faces the crowd that once followed him around and pushed and shoved to get near him. And the crowd, like everyone else, disappoints. And so Jesus will not be spared from a beating that will leave him unrecognizable and a crucifixion that will take his life.

Jesus-level disappointment teaches us that if you are waiting for your friends, or some pastor or leadership, or maybe the government or your social media following to walk you through hopelessness or injustice, you may be waiting listening to awkward cricket noises for a while! If Jesus had to face disappointment with only his Father's plan and the Holy Spirit guiding his feelings, then we shouldn't be shocked when we have to as well. And it was his Father's voice and presence that sustained Jesus in the beating that left him unrecognizable and the crucifixion that stole all hope away from those who believed him to be the Messiah. That's what disappointment does—its steals hope and shifts your perspective. And Jesus's last hours felt hopeless and disappointing.

Jesus was supposed to be the Messiah the Jewish people had dreamed of. Based on the hopes and imaginings of the Jewish people at the time of Jesus's life, Jesus was supposed to come and save them from the Roman occupation. He was supposed to be a military guy, not a hippie who loved people and hung out with the unworthy.

I mean, it was cool he was healing people, but why couldn't he heal himself? The Jewish people who were among the multitudes he fed and healed, I assume, were also disheartened, and I'm pretty sure his disciples and friends were disappointed. Everyone had these expectations of who Jesus was supposed to be and what his reign on the earth was supposed to look like. And none of that ended with a horrible death on a cross. But Jesus, as usual, was unbothered by how everyone perceived him or what they supposed the endgame to be. He happily embraced the struggle and the disappointment and laid down his life on the cross because his only endgame was the purposes and plans of his heavenly Father. Don't miss it. He embraced the struggle, disappointment, and the cross because he had a heavenly perspective.

You can highlight that last sentence—it's how Jesus dealt with feeling disappointed, all while navigating other people's disappointment as well. When the struggle bus shows up, you have every right to feel like life has set you back in some way. But getting on the struggle bus and living disappointed is the complete opposite of what Jesus did, and he is, after all, the compass we need to navigate all our feelings in a healthy way. Jesus walked out disappointment with a viewpoint that understood there is a lesson to be found in our earthly struggles, as the endgame is always rooted in eternity. Jesus knew, regardless of the scars that may have been added to him emotionally and physically, that eternal redemption was always on the other end, regardless of how he felt or how other people felt about the setback.

IF YOU FEEL WOUNDED
BY DISAPPOINTMENT,
ATTACH YOURSELF TO HOPE

Jesus was firmly attached to all his Father was and is and was fully attached to the power of the Holy Spirit. And so, even when he faced the worst disappointment, his feelings and emotions were firmly attached to hope. Jesus modeled this type of attachment to hope so consistently in the storm and wildernesses and potential corners that his disciples were able to model hope even in their despair. Matthew 28 blasts through everyone's chapter 27 grief and unmet expectations with Jesus's resurrection. Hope is alive, and sadly, all these disappointed people focused on their feelings are about to miss it. His disciples have gathered over the weekend, knee-deep in tears and wallowing in the Friday setback they perceived Jesus's death to be. I imagine it looked like a crew of people super sad, living an entire weekend in the same sweatpants, bingeing some show on Netflix, and ordering Five Guys and pizza. And so it was no shock to anyone that, once the Sabbath was over, and in the early hours of that Sunday, only two of Jesus's crew woke up and immediately went to the tomb. Mary Magdalene and the other Mary, the ones who'd experienced the horrors of his death up close, were now hoping to experience his resurrection in the same way.

Matthew says they were going to see the tomb. See what? The rock that was firmly placed in front of the tomb? The Roman guards that were set in place? No, these women went to see hope revealed. They took Jesus at his word about when he would return. Regardless of their feelings—and there were tons of them—regardless of their disappointment, they got up and went to see hope. These were the women who watched Jesus get crucified, and watched him die. They watched everyone's hope for the Messiah pass away and then get dropped from the cross like a rag doll and put in a borrowed tomb. They had all the trauma, all the feelings, and anyone else who'd seen what they had seen would probably be in a corner crying. But hope woke them up early.

Hope woke them up and sent them to the tomb to just see. Regardless of what everyone else was saying and doing, hope inspired them to take Jesus at his word. If you want to overcome disappointment and watch God resurrect your disappointment and despair, get out of your sweatpants and take Jesus at his word. Get up early and seek after his voice, his words, and his ways. Hope is sought after, and once you find it you won't let it go. And these ladies did not let it go.

The trek to the tomb was met with an earthquake, which could have been a deterrent for these women. But it was not; they kept it moving, they kept the pace of peace, and then they arrived to find the soldiers gone, the stone in front of the tomb rolled away, and an angel. "The angel said to the women, 'Do not be afraid, for I know that you are looking for Jesus, who was crucified. He is not here; he has risen, just as he said. Come and see the place where he lay. Then go quickly and tell his disciples: "He has risen from the dead and is going ahead of you into Galilee. There you will see him. Now I have told you"' (Matthew 28:5–7). They were filled with joy and likely totally freaked out—in a good way—and then Jesus showed up!

We see here that hope not only inspired them not to despair, but it kept them seeking. It spoke to their fear and their expectations, answered their questions, and sparked joy. Disappointment kept Jesus's inner circle focused on their grief and at home. His closest friends missed out on this joy-filled moment because they were drowning in the sound of sorrow. Disappointment is loud. It's a snake convo in the garden that overshadows your creator's voice loud. It's the enemy trying to tempt your hunger in a wilderness when you're the most depleted loud. It's your friend who has just died, and even though he said he would make a supernatural comeback, you stayed home and missed the resurrection loud.

The Marys turned the volume of disappointment way down. They were wounded, yes, but they cauterized the bleeding with understanding and hope, and as a result, they found Jesus alive, well, and offering hope. After chatting with the angel, the Bible says that Jesus appeared to them on their way back to the disciples. They immediately grabbed hold of him and began to worship him! If you find yourself disappointed in the middle of a perceived setback, and you haven't sought out Jesus or grabbed on to Jesus in worship, you will miss out on joy and hope in the middle of your disappointment. Hope found in Jesus is tangible, and the Marys experienced that tangible hope in the risen Jesus—and so can we.

When you seek Jesus out in the middle of a setback, you will find him. You just may have to navigate some emotional shaking and other people's grief, but get up anyway and seek him out. Joy is on the other side. I know that disappointment has a way of keeping us asleep in our disappointment and missing out on supernatural resurrection moments. But if you can get past your emotions with facts, you'll be able to see that there is a plan and purpose beyond disappointment. Grab hold of Jesus and worship him, because when you do, you will be filled with hope, perspective, and joy.

You'll be filled with so much joy; in fact, you'll find yourselves affecting your inner circle and encouraging them to seek out Jesus as well. They didn't just experience Jesus for themselves; they went back and told Peter and John. They set the great commission, found in Matthew 28:16–20, in motion. Jesus lived his entire life navigating emotions at the pace of peace and walking in the power of the Holy Spirit, but not so we could model his life alone. He did it so we could be entrusted with walking others through

the garden corners,

the hidden corners,

the wilderness corners,

the follow-me corners,

the crowded corners,

the storm and people-filled corners,

the corners laced with Judas and Peter,

and the corners that feel like torture and death.

The Marys were the first to do this after the resurrection because they got up and didn't allow their scars and sorrow to steal their heavenly perspective or dumb down Jesus's promise to return. And that's how we should live our lives as well, stewarding our feelings like Jesus and lovingly modeling the same pace to others so they can do the same. I know these chapters are heavy, but let me reiterate this truth that I have not missed in writing these pages. The same Jesus who went to scripture when he was experiencing the worst pain ever and was okay with unmet expectations knows you have tons of feelings, as he has tons of feelings. He gets it; life is hard enough, but navigating your emotions doesn't have to be.

I understand the sea of life is a storm magnet filled with panicked people working through their roller coasters and unwanted cave excursions. But God is always with us, always calling us back to his rest and his pace. He is always close and available to lead us into a wilderness filled with healthy emotions to be had and a Holy Spirit to be encountered. The Bible shows us clearly that Jesus's life was not easy. But not easy doesn't make it not worth it. All the struggle, all the emotions—it was all worth it in the end. And no matter what you are walking through or what unhealthy emotion is trying to creep into your heart and mind, know that you are not alone. You have help. There is always a way to pull your heart and mind out of unhealthy feelings, especially disappointment, and that is through Jesus. If you want to walk this life out unbothered by disappointment's noise and others' unmet expectations:

Engage a heavenly perspective.

Embrace your scars.

Assess the wounds.

Stop the bleeding.

Learn all the lessons.

Take Jesus at his word.

Be at peace.

Onward.

CHAPTER 10

HIS PEACE

How to deal with what's next

**Feeling peace is nice; living in
Shalom is a state of being.**

The life of Jesus wasn't just heaven's master plan to restore God's original intent with humanity. The life of Jesus is a practical model for healthy emotional living. It's not an easy fix or a click of our heels that returns us to a non-emotional state; it's a lifestyle of peace that is woven and grafted in with the ways, the truth, and the life of Jesus. And when we engage the model Jesus gave us, we are able to strategically walk out of circumstances and peopling and struggle with a clear guide through those corners that keep us bound in our feelings, even when life is emotionally difficult and unfair, and even when we are working through the worst pain in our life.

True story: while writing this book, I had a medical emergency that hustled me through almost every one of these emotions in an unhealthy way. I woke up in the middle of the night feeling a pain in my side that went from uncomfortable to me sobbing in a corner in less than thirty minutes. When the pain started, I immediately began to pray and speak scriptures about healing over my body. Not because I think Jesus is magical, but because I could feel the overwhelm pulsing through my veins, and I needed to center myself. Also, I believe Jesus is a healer; it says so in the Bible, and it's been something I've seen in my real life. I needed his voice, so I called on it. And in seeking Jesus, I felt the nudge from the Holy Spirit to wake up my husband, as I was going to need a doctor and a hospital visit for this specific pain. Total honesty, when I felt the nudge, I mumbled in the dark, "Nah, Holy Spirit, you got this one, it's one a.m. and I'd like to go back to bed." It was like all I heard was silence, and my immediate healing didn't happen, so I woke up the husband after all, and then I engaged the Holy Spirit and scriptures to calm my mind and my heart.

It makes me think about Jesus's last hours crying in the garden, standing in front of the priests, and then his silence in front of Pilate, and then the crowd. None of those moments made God less God; they just showed us how obedient and calm and focused Jesus really was. I don't normally look as calm as Jesus, but I also prayed as we got into the car and as my husband looked for a hospital close to our new home. I then felt that same familiar Holy Spirit nudge that reminded me of a conversation I had had with a nurse in our church about the best hospitals in our city. I told my husband the one she'd recommended, and off we went.

I kept engaging the Holy Spirit as I sobbed through the pain and the doctors did the blood work; I reminded myself what the scriptures said about rest and wholeness as I went back to a doctor for more blood work and testing. For clarity's sake, when I say I was in pain, this was the worst pain of my life. And I have had major intestinal surgeries and a ruptured appendix! Yet I was not overwhelmed by fear or anxiety. I know, shocking! Based on the previous chapters, I should have yelled at my husband as he tried to comfort me, maybe jumped out of a moving car, and totally asked for some irrational way out of the situation. But I had total peace, even in the pain.

I felt a supernatural peace that kept reminding me that the God who had woken me up, and who told me to wake up my husband, was in the boat and the storm with me. I had peace that kept reminding me that the same God who told me which hospital to go to and who was keeping the pain at a manageable level would not stop speaking to me at that moment. He would not stop pouring out his rest and peace over me as the doctors searched for what was wrong. That peace kept my anxiety and fear at bay, and honestly, so did some very strong pain medicines. Fam, I'm not saying Jesus is the cure-all for all pain and unhealthy emotions; I'm saying Jesus is the route to the cure-all. I am a firm believer that God's word and His Spirit will lead you to

the right help,

the right doctors,

the right hospital,

the right people,

the right church,

the right friends,

the right resources,

and the right therapist.

And if needed, the right meds, when our bodies and minds revolt and our emotions and pain get too much to bear. Jesus and the way he lived is our guide, a road map toward peace and wholeness. Even when the pain feels too much to bear. Even when our emotions rise up to guide our words, our hearts, and our minds, the ways of Jesus are always ready and waiting to take the reins. You just have to choose to walk out that journey with him. One step at a time, at the pace of peace.

GO, BE AT PEACE

In John 20, we find that Jesus's disciples and followers have heard the news of his resurrection, and they are scared and emotional as they gather together. And while they're gathering, Jesus appears in the middle of the room and greets them: "May each one of you be at peace" (John 20:19 VOICE). Here's some context: Jesus has risen, and the word is getting around. Romans and the religious elite think the disciples may have stolen Jesus's body, and it's a dangerous time for the followers of Jesus. Yet they gathered, and Jesus walks into the room. A room full of people who were overwhelmed and fearful because just the thought of Jesus's resurrection being truthful or spoken about could have them all killed. Also, many of those in the room had scattered in the garden of Gethsemane, and I'm sure some of them felt shame and regret on top of the possible fear of death. But now, peace had walked into the room, and peace was what he was bringing to the table.

Jesus walked into the room and didn't say to the masses, filled with fear and shame and regret, *"May each one of you feel at peace."* He said, *"May each one of you **be** at peace."* The same peace that he experienced throughout his walk on earth, he was inviting the room to embrace. He was inviting them to allow *peace to be their identifier* instead of whatever feelings or emotions were drowning them. Also, Jesus used the Hebrew word *Shalom* when he said peace; it's so much more vast than the English word. *Shalom* means *peace*, but it also means safety and rest, wholeness, fullness, soundness, and completion. It's all-encompassing.

Jesus was saying to a room of frightened people he loved, *You have to choose to believe this. You have to choose to pause your feelings and shift to the facts.* It's not that your feelings aren't real and warranted, but he wants us to filter our feelings through him, through love, through peace. Think of it as a water filter that purifies the water before you drink it. That's what Shalom does. It filters your feelings and removes bitterness and unforgiveness and worry and confusion. It assesses the wounds and stops the bleeding. Jesus understood being wounded by people. That's why he showed his wounds. His Shalom doesn't ignore your wounds or help you calm your emotions on a whim. The pace of peace, true Shalom, knows that you have wounds but gives you safety and rest and a shade from unhealthy emotions that wounds may cultivate.

God is always in the room with us. His voice and his presence are always in pocket ready to engage us. Always ready to say, "Come to Me, all who are weary and heavily burdened [by religious rituals that provide no peace], and I will give you rest [refreshing your souls with salvation]. Take My yoke upon you and learn from Me [following Me as My disciple], for I am gentle and humble in heart, and *you will find rest* (renewal, blessed quiet) *for your souls.* For My yoke is easy [to bear] and My burden is light" (Matthew 11:28–30 AMP, emphasis added). His words and his pace are always ready to walk us through struggle; he is here inviting us into Shalom. We just have to accept it and walk it out with him and at his pace.

Shalom is not a feeling but a state of being. When Jesus said to *be* at peace, he wasn't saying feel tranquil or don't feel scared anymore. He was inviting the room to rest their emotions, their thoughts, and their feelings and embrace peace in its fullness. He was saying peace is so much more than you realize, and if you want to win in the next, you must first embrace *Shalom*, the type of peace that doesn't just feel like rest but shows you how to rest. The type of peace that doesn't just feel like wholeness but walks you toward wholeness. The type of peace that doesn't just feel safe but shows you the safeguards found in the power of the Holy Spirit, communion with God the Father, and within the scriptures.

Again, Shalom doesn't mean their other feelings weren't valid or that you won't need help to work through yours; it just means that Jesus is ready and available to help them work through it.

But what does this look like practically? It looks like engaging God's voice when you're overwhelmed, because when his voice is the loudest, peace has room to abide in your thoughts and mind. And the disciples in this part of the Jesus story needed peace to walk into the room and be the loudest voice.

I've said this numerous times throughout these pages—peace isn't something we feel; it's something we receive and live out. You need to get this. If you only want to feel peace to help you navigate your emotions, you're missing out on all the Prince of Peace has to offer you. His peace wasn't rooted in a feeling; it was rooted in a state of being led by the Holy Spirit, ingrained in the scriptures, and in constant communication with his heavenly Father. The Prince of Peace invites you to do the same. He invites you to know his word and his ways. And not in ways based on hearsay, or religious affiliation, but by a covenant and relationship with him. And when that relationship is genuinely activated, feelings bow to unhealthy responses and instead respond in love, peace, joy, patience, and the like.

The disciples were full of fear. Their rabbi and friend had been brutally murdered and now he was there right in front of them, and fear and insecurity had to vanish. When we start to drown in feelings that cause unhealthy responses or we get stuck in emotional quicksand, it's because we aren't walking out our lives with Jesus's point of view. And when that happens, our motives get corrupted, and we lose the ability to read the room. Jesus didn't die a horrible death to restore you to unhealthiness, but to Shalom, to peace. And he did this so you could be love in your everyday life and help others along the path as well.

Jesus referenced this peace, this Shalom, not just once but twice in this text, and I don't think it's a coincidence. The hours before this appearance had been scary, and the days that preceded it were traumatic, exhausting, and overwhelming. But Jesus was not going to leave the community that he loved unprepared. He would not leave the people he had sacrificed his life for without the key to navigating feelings and emotions well. John 20:21 (VOICE) says, "I give you the gift of peace. In the same way the Father sent Me, I am now sending you." Jesus was about to leave and ascend back to heaven, and Shalom was his parting gift. Jesus was about to deploy his community, his friends, his family, and his disciples into the world to be love and model joy and patience, compassion, and self-control, but first, they needed to *be* at peace. The type of peace that understood peace was more than a feeling, but a state of wholeness and rest solely found in the Prince of Peace and ready to follow the ways of Jesus closely, embracing solitude and walking in the power of the Holy Spirit.

GO HOME

When you walk out your faith connected to Jesus fully, your life becomes a beacon of hope and health to others. Not through religious traditions, but by the way you love others. By the way you function from a place of Shalom, joy, and goodness. Some of the people in my life who have modeled this for me the best are not the people who go to church every week, or who preach from pulpits. They are the unknowns, the ones I believe Jesus would have snatched up for his crew. And those are the people God sent out to change the world. "I give you the gift of peace. In the same way the Father sent Me, I am now sending you." He is sending you out, but he can't send you out an emotional mess. He can use an emotional mess, but he won't send an emotional mess. We see this when Jesus goes back to Nazareth to mature in the Matthew 2 story, and then we see it again when he bypasses the emotional people in Luke 8 to stop and heal the woman with the issue of bleeding.

There is a story in Matthew 8 about a man named Legion that follows the Jesus sleeping on a pillow story. I referenced it in the Pace chapter. He was legit scary, and he's who met the disciples on the shore after the storm and panic of emotions that Jesus calmed with his words. They called him Legion because he had a legion of demons hanging out with him. He was also living in a cemetery and naked, wearing nothing but the chain and irons someone tried to strap onto him. Everything about this man spoke to his brokenness, yet Jesus saw someone worthy of sending. I'm not saying that if you are emotional, you're full of demons; I'm saying people who are run solely by how they feel will come across as looking like Legion and scaring people. Being unfiltered and emotionally naked doesn't make you honest or avant-garde; it makes you look immature. When people used to get offended by things I said, I used to tell them that they didn't understand me or my culture, or I blamed it on being creative. I chalked it up to people not understanding my vibe or my level of honesty. But I was just young, and I didn't know how to articulate my thoughts or read the room. I also didn't have the right circle to help me and keep me accountable. The truth is, my emotions weren't bad or invalid; it was just that how I filtered them was bad, and so I invalidated them with my responses and my actions. If the only thing people have ever experienced about you is your hefty emotions, they are missing the best of you. Jesus wants to send you out on the path toward wholeness and walking in Shalom.

When the man in Luke 8, Legion, experienced Jesus, he found wholeness and Shalom, and he asked Jesus if he could go with him. Which sounds legit. Jesus could have added another friend to his crew. But Jesus told him no, he said, "Return home and tell how much God has done for you." Before Jesus sends you out to reflect his love and Shalom, he sends you home. Home will be the best place for you to practice healthy emotions. Legion went home and impacted his city as well. But if you don't start at home with your spouse, with your kids, or with whoever is closest to you, the citywide impact will be fleeting. If you are only good and calm outside your home and then you get home and unleash your feelings on your closest people, then you're doing this whole Shalom thing all wrong. Living at the pace of Jesus and embracing peace should start at home. Start in the private places of your life, in your alone time, the moments you don't post on social media. Work out your emotions there, and then when life throws stuff at you, you respond from peace. We live in a culture that glorifies public platforms and acclaim over privacy and peace. And Jesus sent this guy home because what he needed was peace, not a platform. Go home and practice peace, especially in your home, as the home is sacred.

Peace matters in my home. It's my life goal to have a home full of Shalom. When our family and friends come to visit, they say our house always feels so peaceful, and that they sleep the best when they are at our house. And every time someone says it, my heart leaps out of my chest with joy because I fight for the peace to rest in our home. In 2021 we moved to a new city to pastor a community, and we bought a new home. The first thing we did when we arrived was pray for peace over our new city. And then we walked our new home and anointed the corners of each room and prayed for peace to fill the home. Not in a religious way, but in a sacred way.

We wanted God to know that our home was his to do with what he wanted and we were preparing it for him. We were setting a table for God to walk in and join our lives, and everything we did and launched from this home. We were saying, "God, this is your house; do with it what you will." We even placed a mezuzah on the main doorpost so that when others enter our home they understand this house belongs to the Lord. We play worship music throughout the day, we honor the Sabbath, and we fill our home with people as much as possible. We want our home and our lives to be a respite of peace, so we consistently invite God into the room.

Just like I fight for peace in my home, I fight for peace in my mind and my heart. Our hearts and minds are the resting place for emotions. They are the sacred spaces I invite God into as I want to make sure I'm healthy and expressing Shalom in my emotions. God can't send me to be love if I first don't love myself and the people already entrusted to me in my words and in my actions. As the church, the establishment, it feels like we've done such a great job of sending people out to make disciples, share the Gospel, and launch churches, yet we somehow stopped sending people home to grow in favor with God and man. I believe if we started sending people home first, there would be fewer people crying in corners. There would be fewer people with church hurt, and more people understanding who Jesus is and was.

We have stopped looking at home as a place of peace; it's just a place we do laundry before we head back out to make disciples. But Jesus understood home, and that's why he went back to his disciples when he was resurrected instead of heading straight for the masses. He went back to his inner circle and community. If you want to stop crying in the corners of life, go home and build up a home that is full of love and peace. And if you do, then God can entrust you to go out and be love, produce love, and express love. But it's only when you first embrace Shalom with your families and community that he can entrust you with more people.

GO, MAKE DISCIPLES

When I was a kid growing up in the eighties, we spent countless Halloweens passing out tracts at the door instead of candy. One year my youth group picketed a Marilyn Manson concert.

I remember being super embarrassed. Nothing about those scenarios expressed the love of Jesus the way I had experienced it. It just made people feel dumb and unwanted by God. It spoke to religious rules and traditions, and it told the people we encountered they were failing. It said nothing about the love of God who sent his only Son to sacrifice his life for humanity. When Jesus sent out his disciples to impact the nations and share his good news of salvation, the expectation was that they would model and express love the way Jesus did, not that they would go out and tell everyone they were less than, because they weren't living the life the way Jesus intended.

Jesus's way of making disciples was saturated in truth and love. It looked like walking along a shore and inspiring four young fishermen to follow him, with intentionality and joy. Jesus went out and found people; it was active and patient. He went out to the highways and byways and loved a crazy guy with demons in tow because his version of making disciples looked like gentleness and compassion. Jesus went out and healed the hand of a man whom no one thought was worthy to be healed on the Sabbath. And that compassion and unhurried pace caused Jesus to stop and heal and encourage a woman who'd been suffering for twelve years! Even when everyone told him to keep moving.

He even reminded Judas, his betrayer, that he had a purpose when everyone else probably wished for some form of retaliation. Jesus looked at redemption and loving people differently. And he looked at emotions very differently than we do. When he faced the most disappointing and scary circumstances, he responded with peace and love. He did this because his emotions were filtered through his Father's voice, the presence of the Holy Spirit, and the truths he modeled out of the scriptures. Healthy emotions aren't just something we strive after for our personal well-being, but they are also launching pads that God uses to bless and help other people.

How do you express the love of Jesus? Is it active in your everyday life and in your home, or is it only on Sundays? Are you passing out tracts or picketing those who don't believe what you believe, or are you seeing people the way Jesus did? In Jesus's time, the people who were thought of as the worst of the worst were the tax collectors. They were the ones everyone thought of as the biggest sinners, and yet we see Jesus added a tax collector to his twelve. Matthew was a young Jewish tax collector. He wasn't just hated by the religious and used by the Romans, but his own people detested him for having that job. He had no community, yet Jesus included him in his.

Making disciples isn't just inviting someone to church or asking them to join a group; it's inviting them into your life. Jesus didn't invite Matthew to follow him to his speaking gigs, but to follow him closely as a friend. God can't entrust you with people if your life is an emotional mess. God can't entrust you to pull Matthews close if you aren't filtering your life and emotions through his ways, his life, and his truth. In a culture where everyone has their own personal truth, Jesus is inviting you into his, as it's the only way to an emotionally healthy life.

It's an invitation to Shalom that inspires your home toward peace and filters your emotions through

his voice

his presence

his words

his ways

his point of view

his pace

his motives

his discretion

and his peace.

And it's in the following where we truly find health and wholeness and a way to move forward past the crying corners and feelings that drown us on the daily.

GO WITH HELP

You can't walk out this life in the power of the Holy Spirit without holding the hand of Shalom. We see this in Acts 2; there is a gathering, and after the foundation of peace and Shalom is poured, the disciples get together to pray. And when they do, the Holy Spirit comes in like a rushing wind to activate the power of love, joy, peace, patience, kindness, goodness, faithfulness, gentleness, and self-control. Jesus has ascended, and now the comforter, the helper that powered

Jesus up in the wilderness, was there to inspire his people toward love. Those in the room had seen the scriptures lived out by Jesus; they had been given a master class on how to walk out feelings, corners, solitude, hiddenness, and storms. And now, the Holy Spirit had been dropped like a supernatural bomb within the community to help them navigate the next season with healthy emotions.

The Holy Spirit bomb was necessary as it not only activated and deployed Jesus into ministry; it was now going to activate and deploy the followers of Jesus into ministry. And by ministry, I mean loving people like Jesus did with heaven's how-to guide for navigating emotions and hardships. It sent them out with help, and with healthy emotions that would draw others in with love to follow the ways of Jesus. It also sent them out with healthy emotions that would draw others in with compassion to embrace the truth of Jesus. And it sent them out with the healthy emotions that would encourage others with patience to live the life that is only found in Jesus.

You can't be deployed into the world to be love and show the love of Jesus if you are led solely by your emotions and pitching tents in the corners of life. You can't be deployed into your home to bring peace if you are led solely by your emotions and crying in corners. And Jesus wants to deploy you like he did his community in the Bible: with a deep understanding of Shalom and fully activated by the Holy Spirit.

This doesn't happen by only attending a Sunday service once a week or by reading a verse on your phone every morning. This happens by truly living out the ways of Jesus, the truth of Jesus, and the life of Jesus.

Practically speaking, it looks like talking to him throughout your day and ignoring the snakes. It looks like filling up on his words and sitting in his presence. It will look like rooting yourself in who he says you are and not what you feel about yourself or what others say. And it would look like surrendering your zeal, reading the room, and forgiving people who've hurt you. And when life gets too hard, it will look like waking up the right people, putting up the right boundaries, and living at a pace of peace.

What I've written are truths excavated in my own garden moments; they are the principles that I dug up in the hiddenness and in the wilderness, the truths and principles that reminded me of who I am in the caves and in the storms, in my barrenness and in my pain. They are tried and tested "Jesus truths" that have freed me from living hostage to my emotions. Emotions and feelings that were rooted in fear and fertilized by unhealthy people and circumstances. There is no true wholeness, rest, safety, or peace felt or experienced without following Jesus closely. He is the way, the truth, and the life, and you can't experience life to its fullest or emotions in a healthy way without following the one who created you and gave you your emotions.

So let's embrace peace, and let's allow the Holy Spirit to deploy us into the next.

May the Lord bless you and keep you;

May the Lord make his face shine on you and be gracious to you;

May the Lord turn his face toward you and give you peace.

Shalom.

ACKNOWLEDGMENTS

Thank you, Sarah Byrd, for being my friend, for listening to Jesus, and for coaching me through this book. I would not have completed this book if it wasn't for you. True story!

Thank you, Kaylee Morgan, for reading these chapters before I sent them, making me coffee, doing my laundry, cooking us dinner, and keeping the ball moving during this process. You are a gift to our family.

Thank you to Mrs. Pam Tebow for speaking on my behalf when no one else did. For believing in me when I'd lost hope and inspiring me to chase Jesus in the midst of my feelings.

To Nik Goodner, who spoke into existence the platform for *I Cry in Corners*. I am forever thankful for your kindness and trust.

Thank you, DeAnn Carpenter, for texting me often and randomly during this process and reminding me of how sacred it was.

Thank you, Kyle Negrete and the team at the Fedd Agency, for emailing me back when other agents didn't respond or believe in me. Thank you for your trust and seeing my heart and the heart of the message.

And finally, to Beth Adams, for your beautifully tough love that pushed this book forward when I wholeheartedly wanted to give up, and cry in a corner, in my kitchen, and in my sweatpants. You are the Yoda of writing, and I'm grateful that you stuck with me.

ABOUT THE AUTHOR

Chari Orozco (*pronounced Cha-dee*) is an author of books, teacher of the Bible, and podcaster focused on all the feels. She is passionate about sharing the love of Jesus and using her gifts of speaking, writing, and design to impact the lives of those around her. When Chari is not writing or teaching, she can be found reading too many books at once, walking through a museum, and drinking way too much coffee. She also serves with her husband as lead pastors of Hope St. Pete in St. Petersburg, Florida.